Lit *from* Within

Lit *from* Within

A SIMPLE GUIDE TO THE
ART OF INNER BEAUTY

Victoria Moran

HarperSanFrancisco
A Division of HarperCollinsPublishers

HarperCollins books may be purchased for educational, business, or sales
promotional use. For information please write: Special Markets Department,
HarperCollins Publishers, Inc., 10 East 53rd Street, New York, NY 10022.

HarperCollins Web site: http://www.harpercollins.com

HarperCollins®, 📖®, and HarperSanFrancisco™ are trademarks of
HarperCollins Publishers, Inc.

FIRST HARPERCOLLINS PAPERBACK EDITION PUBLISHED IN 2004.

Designed by Jessica Shatan

Library of Congress Cataloging-in-Publication Data
Moran, Victoria.
Lit from within : a simple guide to the art of inner beauty / Victoria Moran.
p. cm.
        Includes bibliographical references.
ISBN 0–06–251734–1 (pbk.)
1. Beauty, Personal. 2. Women—Psychology. 3. Women—Attitudes. 4. Body
image in women. 5. Mind and body. 6. Yoga. I. Title.
HQ1219.M64 2001
305.4—dc21   00–054056

04 05 06 07 08 QUE(M) 10 9 8 7 6 5 4 3 2 1

To Adair, as you spread your wings,

and to William,

for loving me enough to

help me do some flying of my own

CONTENTS

Part III ✍ Body and Soul

Part IV ✍ Just for Fun

Part V ✍ Quality of Life

INTRODUCTION

When you realize that you are indeed "fearfully and wonderfully made," you can get over worrying so much about your thighs and your crow's-feet and start bowling people over with your presence.

Your physical self is by no means the totality of who you are. It does, however, *reflect* who you are: a unique spiritual being of extraordinary beauty and importance. When you understand this and you see yourself in this way, you will treat your body as if it housed a soul, and you will live your life as though it were part of a grand design. You will be rewarded with an unmistakable radiance that comes from deep within and shows on the outside, too.

If you talk with large numbers of luminous women, as I have, you will find that in one way or another they all "got religion." Life prompted them—often through pain, sometimes through joy—to look for hidden truths beneath the surface of their circumstances. Some deepened their childhood faith; others found a new one. Many discovered prayer or meditation, or they got over an addiction or out of a quandary by rebuilding their lives on a spiritual foundation.

Whatever the particulars, a power entered their lives that caused their self-centered concerns to shrink and their hearts to grow. You can call this power God, and I do that sometimes in this book. If another word works better for you, by all means use it. Whatever name you choose, this is a power that can elevate your thoughts and diminish the ones that obscure your inner light: fear, jealousy, anger, greed—you know, the basic seven deadlies and some pesky hangers-on.

Being perfect is unnecessary. Being human will do. When you realize that you are indeed "fearfully and wonderfully made," you can get over worrying so much about your thighs and your crow's-feet and start bowling people over with your *presence*. You don't have to look like the women in the magazines. They usually represent one idea of beauty, an idea dependent on youth and abetted by cosmetics, lighting, and the art of the touch-up. What you'll have instead is a glow that can be neither bought nor bottled.

Until quite recently, contemporary culture didn't put much stock in having a lovely soul. This was probably because nobody could figure out how to make a profit from it. Whatever the reason, that message to devalue the beauty that arises from deep within crept into the collective consciousness. In reality, though, inner beauty is the only kind that truly matters because it's the only kind that goes the distance.

You can think of its outward expression as charisma or grace, as class or poise. When you have it, your eyes really are windows to the soul. Your smile can put anyone at ease. An irresistible attraction emanates from your personality so that, regardless of your age or body type, and regardless of whether you think of yourself as pretty or not, you *are* beautiful. It is a matter of developing the soul, the bridge that connects you as a body-mind entity with the spirit, the inner light, "that of God in every person." This is the radiance that can light up a room, and light up your life.

The purpose of this book is to help you recognize the inner light that the people who care about you already see and to open the channels for even more of that light to express itself. For *Lit from Within* to benefit you most, adopt the following as a working hypothesis while you're reading the essays and trying out the recommendations in them:

1. Inner beauty is a real and valuable commodity.

2. You yourself have it in spades.

3. You can take simple, practical actions to make your inner beauty more visible to yourself and others.

The book is divided into eight sections that address different ways to enable you to connect more fully with the beauty inside you. They are:

1. *Attitude*—looking at your physical and spiritual self in a way that invites your inner light to shine;

2. *Actions*—things to do right now to look more beautiful—and live more beautifully—from the inside out;

3. *Body and Soul*—the connection between that part of you that looks back from the mirror and the essence behind it;

4. *Just for Fun*—the playful side of looking and feeling radiant;

5. *Quality of Life*—extending your beauty out into myriad aspects of your life;

6. *Quality of Character*—setting standards and striving to reach them;

7. *Nourishing Yourself*—taking care of yourself physically, with good food, water, and air, and spiritually through the ambience that surrounds your meals;

8. *Nurturing Your Spirit*—the big picture: how to trust, stay close to your values, and realize the interconnectedness of all that is.

Don't feel obligated to read every chapter, or even every section, in order. "Jumping around" may be what you need to customize this book to your specific needs.

However you read it, here is my promise: there is no exclusivity when it comes to being lit from within. There exists inside every one of us unimaginable light and energy and beauty— what Robert Browning called "the imprisoned splendor." Each suggestion on the following pages, whether you'd label it a spiritual exercise, a practical action, or a lighthearted diversion, is designed to impress you with this, your true identity. As long as you can remember who you really are, in the midst of the world's expectations about what you're supposed to be, the light that is in you already will take care of the rest.

PART I

Attitude

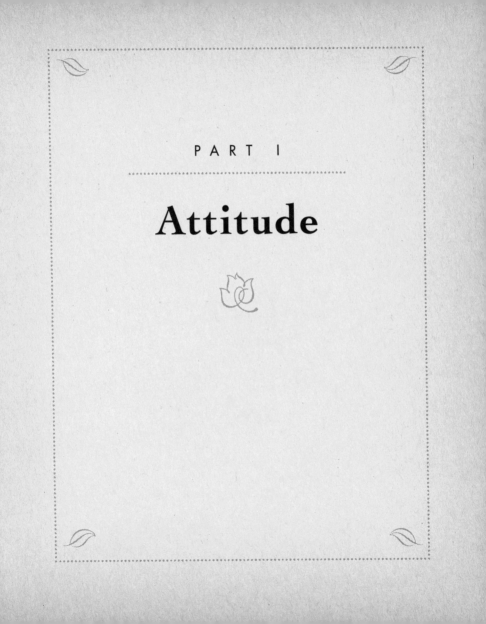

1

Let Your Exterior Reflect Your Interior

The first step toward bringing out your inner beauty is to have only one goal for your physical self: that it be an accurate representation of your spiritual self.

When the light of your spirit shows on your face and in your life, you are a beautiful human being, a beautiful woman. For this to happen in an enduring way, you need to take exceptionally good care of both your body and your soul. You just have to get the order right: the soul came first. A new theory edging its way into science is that of "enformy," the notion that something—what religious people have long known as soul—exists prior to the formation of a physical body. This immaterial essence "enforms" matter, resulting in something magnificent—you, for instance.

In opting to take on physical form, your spiritual self didn't make any mistakes. The body you've got is the one you're

supposed to have. From the vantage point of your soul, it is
the perfect body to carry you through this lifetime and accomplish what you came here to do. And whether your body type
is the delicate ectomorph, the curvaceous endomorph, or the
athletic mesomorph, you're "morphed" just the way you're
supposed to be.

This can be hard to swallow in a culture that suggests—no,
shouts—that certain bodies are acceptable and others are not.
The message these days is that women are supposed to be tall
and thin and have large breasts. When I was a teenager, they
were supposed to be tall and thin and have no breasts. When
my grandmother was young, Clara Bow was the "It Girl," and
five-foot-two and curvy was the ideal.

Whatever a particular era's "perfect body" is supposed to
look like, its purpose (detailed in Linda McBryde's *The Mass
Market Woman*) is to sell things: clothes, makeup, beer, movie
tickets. Your body, however, has a higher calling: to give your
soul, your light within, a way to show itself in the world. This
undertaking is supposed to entail more ecstasy than agony. The
Vedic scriptures of ancient India say that human bodies were
engineered to experience bliss and that even the angels envy
them.

The first step toward bringing out your inner beauty is to
have only one goal for your physical self: that it be an accurate
representation of your spiritual self. Unlike the defeatist goals of
the "lose ten pounds" school, this one is freeing. You're giving
yourself permission to be precisely who you were meant to be,
externally as well as internally. Once you let go of all objectives

for your body other than to have it express your essential self, you allow it, along with your mind and spirit, to work for the good of the whole. If being ten pounds lighter is part of that overall good, it will happen. And it will last.

When you are committed to showing the world who you really are, you will start to play up what makes you special. Actress Bette Midler has been quoted as saying, "If only I'd known that one day my differentness would be an asset, my early life would have been much easier." If you celebrate your differentness, the world will, too. It believes exactly what you tell it—through the words you use to describe yourself, the actions you take to care for yourself, and the choices you make to express yourself. Tell the world that you are a one-of-a-kind creation who came here to experience wonder and spread joy. Expect to be accommodated.

2

Think Well of Yourself

Perceived worth determines value, and value necessitates care.

It's likely that you already have a leg up on nurturing the beauty of your soul: you're *nice* to your soul. You may be less gracious to your body. Almost no one says, "My soul is a mess." They're too busy ridiculing their hips or their hair. Your inner beauty cannot show on the outside, however, unless you think well of yourself, the whole and all of its parts.

If you don't believe you're worth taking care of, you won't do it—at least not for long. Perceived worth determines value, and value necessitates care. For instance, let's say you go to a yard sale and pick up a set of dishes for fifteen dollars—spares to have on hand for a picnic or a potluck. But your friend who knows about antiques sees your tag-sale find and tells you,

"These are rare antiques of the Worth-a-Lot pattern. You could get five thousand dollars for them now, and their value is going up by the day." What are you going to do? Probably start taking better care of those dishes.

Something similar happens when you place a higher value on yourself. You naturally want to care for what you prize, your body and soul included. When you hold yourself in this esteem, you'll know intuitively what actions to take. You'll develop an acute sense of life balance, so you will quickly discern when some part of you needs attention. You will have time for physical exercise, mental rest, and personal treats because your priorities will change. You won't have to work it all out in your day planner; it will happen automatically because of the value shift that has taken place.

One very practical way to increase your standing in your own mind is to refrain from comparing yourself to other people or fabrications of people (airbrushed, retouched enhancements of women who, first thing in the morning, look a lot like the rest of us). This is easier if you call a temporary moratorium on reading magazines or watching TV shows that imply that your age, weight, income, or any other part of who you are today makes you unworthy. Also, abstain from measuring your current self against some earlier edition—back when you were younger, thinner, could afford better clothes, whatever. You are still that person, and she was always you.

If it is still difficult to regard yourself highly without feeling like a fraud, realize that not doing so is a kind of perverse egotism. If practically everybody else on earth (heinous criminals and murderous dictators exempted) is just fine, it's really rather selfish to see yourself as singled out for special, albeit negative, status. You're human. That means top of the line. Shortcomings are an integral part of the package, and overcoming some of them is a wondrous possibility.

3

Give Yourself Positive Messages

Every cell that's in us is a living entity responding to our thoughts and feelings.

M y friend Necia, a massage therapist, never worries about getting sick. "I touch health, I teach health, I give health, I *am* health," she has told me with complete conviction. In the eight years I've known her, I can't remember her being unwell. When we are as convinced of our worth as Necia is of her wellness, we'll be living in new bodies and a new world.

Your mind talks to your body all the time. If it's saying things like "Getting a little flabby there, aren't we?" and "You just took 'bad hair day' to a whole new low," your physical self is taking on heaps of criticism. No living thing can blossom under such a barrage, not a child or a pet or a body. According to the quantum physicists, every cell—indeed every atom—that's in us is a *living entity* responding to our thoughts and feelings.

Using affirmations is one technique for changing how we think about ourselves and our circumstances. An affirmation is a statement that is true in the grand scheme of things but that may not be an observable fact in our lives right now. For example, "I am an expression of divine beauty and divine love" is a true statement for anyone who wishes to be open to it and depict it in her life. "I am twenty-one and a natural blond" can be true only for certain people; it lacks that grand-scheme application and therefore would not count as an affirmation. Even if you have used affirmations before, compose some for yourself to use while you read this book. Just thinking of them can be uplifting:

- I am beautiful, gracious, content.

- I am the radiant expression of a divine idea.

- I accept my body as it is today and allow it to become even healthier and more beautiful.

- Every day I feel more alive.

- I am excited about experiencing life as a physical being with a divine purpose.

These are powerful words, but for any affirmation to make a difference, you have to counter the brain's built-in bias against new ideas. To do this requires more than repeating words; you have to work with them.

Take some time every day to sit with the idea underlying the words. Mull over the concept. Use the power of your imagination to contemplate scenarios in which this statement could play out in fact. "What would today look like for me if I really saw myself as beautiful, gracious, and content? What would I be doing? What would I have had for breakfast?" Put yourself in that scene. Experience your leg muscles working hard on your morning hike. Feel the softness of the sweater you're wearing. Taste the raspberries you're eating, and see the wildflower bouquet on the table. This is a way to make the words three-dimensional, to midwife a concept into form.

Write your affirmation. Work with only one affirmation at a time. Don't make things complicated. It helps to make two columns—one for the affirmation itself, the other for your brain's response to it. You may have read that writing down a negative statement solidifies it in your consciousness. That is not the case when you write responses to affirmations, no matter how negative they sound. You need to let your cynical side have its say, or it might never let up. Respond to every argument with your affirmation. Eventually, the negative rebuttals lose steam and stop altogether. For example:

I am beautiful.	You're nuts.
I am beautiful.	You're kidding, right?
I am beautiful.	I hate to break it you, but you're not.
I am beautiful.	No, but you're at least average.

I am beautiful.	You did look good the other night.
I am beautiful.	Hmm, it's possible.
I am beautiful.	Uh-huh.
I am beautiful.	I always told you that.

It doesn't happen this fast, but after a few weeks of working with an idea, the brain will let down its barriers and come along with you.

Put reminders of your affirmation all over the place. Stick them on your bathroom mirror, the refrigerator, your checkbook cover, your computer monitor. It's hard to overdo this because your new concept is being challenged on all sides by a world around you that routinely judges by appearances, rates by arbitrary standards, and reflects your old beliefs about yourself back to you.

Don't let your conversing contradict your affirming. You can spend twenty minutes a day reciting, "I am magnificent." You can write it a thousand times and make your apartment look like the National Post-its Museum. But if the first time you misspell a word you say, "I'm so dumb," or if you need a bigger size in the fitting room, you say, "I'm such a pig," that magnificence loses ground.

Speaking well of yourself is simply the audible version of thinking well of yourself. It doesn't mean telling everyone you meet that you're extraordinary, but don't deny it either. Refrain from making yourself unnecessarily small. Say thank you to compliments about your appearance without tagging on a caveat like "I've had this dress for ages." When what you say and what you're trying to bring into being support each other, you cease being at odds with yourself. This is one definition of integrity, and it helps your light shine.

4

Surround Yourself with People Who See Your Light

Perhaps all you need to do to be more fully lit from within is to be around more people who see your light.

To the people who love you, you are beautiful already. This is not because they're blind to your shortcomings but because they so clearly see your soul. Your shortcomings then dim by comparison. The people who care about you are willing to let you be imperfect and beautiful, too.

One Sunday afternoon I went with a friend to a yard sale. The woman holding the sale offered to help us carry some things, but her husband wouldn't hear of it, saying, "Oh, no, sweetie pie, you might break a nail." He did the carrying himself. To anyone else who saw her that day, "sweetie pie" looked like an unkempt woman wearing too much blusher and not enough halter. To the man who loved her, however, she was striking. We all need people who see us at our best even when we aren't. Having a life partner this enamored is a blessing but not a requirement. Friends and family who think the world of us are a great gift, too.

Think about the potential members of your fan club. If you have a child or grandchild under eight, you've got one member for sure. Discover the others by thinking about friends and family members whom you hold in this kind of positive regard. Do you have a friend or two or several who may not have seemed terribly attractive when you met them but who now look absolutely beautiful to you? That's because you've come to see their light. Chances are, if you're seeing theirs, they're seeing yours.

Perhaps all you need to do to be more fully lit from within is to be around more people who see your light. If a friend sees your human limitations more clearly than your divine gifts, you don't need that friend. If a co-worker can't see your light, you might consider moving to a different department or a another part of the office if you can. And certainly if the person making you feel "less than" is a stranger—someone who has written a magazine article or is giving advice on the radio—turn the page or change the station.

It gets more complicated when our biggest detractors are key players in our lives. Sometimes we married them or we share parents with them. With these people, it's important to keep quiet about what you're doing. Let your light shine, regardless of who sees it and who refuses to. Think well of yourself, in spite of the fact that someone close to you doesn't. And affirm like crazy, even as a silent response to a subtle slur. Once you truly value yourself, that person will, too, or risk losing his place or her place in your life.

Sometimes the voices listing your liabilities belong to people who are no longer a part of your life but whose opinions of you helped shape your own. When these musty memories rise to the surface—as they will when you take steps to see your innate wonder—tell them, "No thanks. This is outmoded information." If someone handed you a piece of carbon paper when you had ready access to a copy machine, you would say no. You don't need antiquated technology when you have something more efficient. And you don't need old messages about who you are when you have new and better ones. The Reverend Chris Michaels once told his congregation, "The people who abused you didn't know who they were dealing with." Once you know, everything changes.

5

Let Other Women Be Beautiful, Too

People who think only a model type can be a beautiful woman are as lacking in sophistication as those who think only a burger and fries can be a tasty meal.

Let other women be beautiful, too. Let them have beautiful bodies and beautiful lives. The fact that anyone has either is evidence that the universe is eager to pass out perks. Your inner light will have a hard time making inroads in how you look and feel if you envy one woman's image or another's success, the love in this one's life or the ease of that one's. They're supposed to have their blessings, and you're supposed to have yours. You'll have even more of them when you freely, openly, and without hesitation allow other women their good fortune, whether it comes across as a fat bank account, a slim figure, or whatever else seems enticing and out of your reach.

When we want to be what someone else is or have what someone else has, we insult Providence with the implication that there isn't enough to go around. A beauty treatment worth more than any exfoliating facial or Asian seaweed wrap is to be genuinely happy for another woman's good fortune. (I say "another woman's" because most of us seldom envy children or men. We place them in another category, as if we have to compete for crumbs from a finite store of luck earmarked for females over eighteen.)

When you celebrate someone else's success, you get to fill your body and soul with the boon of positive emotion. Even if this isn't the day your personal ship comes in, showing up for the docking of someone else's lets you partake of the physical and spiritual rewards of joy and unselfishness. Moreover, because the thoughts we have today draw tomorrow's experiences to us, celebrating another's success can only bring us more of the same.

It works with physical appearance, too. We have to allow other women to be beautiful, both those who are widely regarded as such and those who aren't. The ones who are ravishing by current standards have in that both a blessing and a curse. Being dazzlingly attractive means attracting everything and everybody, positive and negative, good and bad. Women whose beauty is not readily apparent have a hard time, too. Perhaps in another era or another culture, they would be the goddesses. As it is, they're considered ordinary, but of course they're not. God has made every sort of human being, but there hasn't been an ordinary one yet.

You see the beauty in others the same way you see it in yourself: by looking beyond appearances to the person living in the body and the spirit that animates both. Conversely, you're never more beautiful to another person than when you regard him or her in this light. This is how people look at us when they love us very much. It's also how people of true spiritual depth look at everyone. It's happened to you, I'm sure: someone looks at you with such pure love, such positive regard, it goes straight to your soul. A lovely ideal is to behold all people, friends and strangers, in this way. Remind yourself:

There is enough to go around—enough beauty, enough joy, enough success. No one can take yours from you, so applaud other people's.

Standing next to somebody stunning will not make you look less so. In fact, beauty is like good lighting; you look better when you're near it.

Somebody thinks everybody is beautiful. This is why the football captain and the homecoming queen aren't the only people from your high school who got married. See with bigger eyes. See subtle beauty and spiritual beauty.

People are gifted in different ways, but we're all gifted. Some women look beautiful to men; others look beautiful to cameras; we all look beautiful to those who know us well enough to see our souls.

You have the responsibility to intervene when people around you put others down for how they look. This kind of juvenile behavior should end by seventh grade. Unfortunately, it doesn't. Whether the unkind remarks are because someone is too attractive or not attractive enough, speak up on the absent person's behalf.

There are myriad types of beauty. People who think only a model type can be a beautiful woman are as lacking in sophistication as those who think only a burger and fries can be a tasty meal.

Segregation is an evil because it keeps us from seeing who another person really is. We're finally getting past racial segregation, but we still segregate ourselves terribly by age, income, and looks. Most people only have friends who are at their approximate level of attractiveness based on societal standards. I'm not suggesting that you make a token friend who is drop-dead gorgeous and another who might be considered ugly, but when you meet someone of either description, give her the same chance to be your friend as you would someone who seems to be more "in your league."

All people deserve to be treated the same way: with respect. Studies have shown that plain people are passed over for hiring and promotions, and yet no one hates them for looking the way they do. Attractive people, on the other hand, are treated well to their faces but often denounced behind their backs. Start where you are to make the nonsense on both sides stop. Begin with fair and equal treatment of your children and their friends, yourself and your friends, and even the celebrities we've never met but love to talk about. Let them be beautiful. Allow them to flourish. Join them in living well.

6

Have an Ageless Outlook

*You grow into what you envision. If you think of sixty as
young, you'll be a young sixty; if you believe that eighty
means decrepit, your body is already working to
accommodate your belief.*

The age issue is tricky and I have a sense that I'll know a lot
more about it the farther along I get. I do know that we confuse the natural changes brought by time with the unnecessary
ones wrought by abuse. Western culture's infatuation with youth
muddies the waters even more. It discounts people, women in particular, just when they've attained enough wisdom to be most
highly regarded. The youth obsession also has nothing to do with
the soul, which grows more beautiful as time passes, or with the
inner light, which exists beyond space and time and is not affected
by them.

Besides, many characteristics we attribute to youth—enthu-
siasm, vitality, fitness—speak less of age than attitude. We owe

it to ourselves to maintain these qualities as long as we can. This is not the same as looking eighteen indefinitely. It's better— not to mention possible. The bloom of youth is, of course, wonderful. We're supposed to revel in it when we have it. A pimple or a bad hair day or an extra few pounds could never diminish the powerful charm that comes with simply being young. Contrary to popular belief, however, true beauty doesn't stop there; youth is merely the starting point from which it evolves.

People live longer and better now than ever, yet many of us feel traumatized when we turn thirty, forty, and fifty as if we lived in the days when thirty was old, forty ancient, and fifty dead. In our day, God willing, you're here for an extended stay, and you will pass through many stages. Live each one to the fullest, and discover the gifts it offers. Adapt as your body changes, and you grow into a more seasoned but still exquisite version of yourself. Certainly if you want to take advantage of cosmetic and medical means available to look younger, you have every right to do so. Your maturity is supposed to show through your actions; it doesn't all have to show on your face. Just don't try so hard that it backfires. A mature woman with a fit body and a nice complexion is lovely; another the same age who's been tucked and pulled in every direction can be pitiful.

Then there are women like Phyllis who, without benefit of surgery, belie their age to an astounding degree. I met Phyllis at one of my workshops and assumed she was perhaps sixty and in quite good shape. I was shocked to learn that she was eighty-two. When I asked her secret, she said, "I was brought up with the understanding that there is much more light in the world than darkness. Since I know that, I simply don't allow negative things in."

It hit me like a truckload of hair color and alpha-hydroxy cream: Phyllis is not extraordinarily youthful for eighty-two; she is the way eighty-two was meant to be. She may have good genes, but her attitude has enabled them to reach their potential. To increase your odds for being like Phyllis when you're her age, start today to think the way Phyllis thinks. Worry, fear, faultfinding, resentment, and regret accelerate the negative aspects of aging—perhaps by making life so unpleasant you'd prefer to hurry and get it over with. Instead, look for the good until you find it. See the bright side of a gloomy situation. If there isn't one, think about *anything* that lifts your spirits. If you do this, people will describe you as happy. Let them. "Brooding" and "dramatic" only sound more interesting, and they age you faster than chain-smoking and tanning beds.

To some degree at least, you grow into what you envision. If you think of sixty as young, you're likely to be a young sixty; if you believe that eighty means decrepit, your body is already working to accommodate your belief. So think occasionally of the woman you will be years and years from now. Befriend her and see her in a lovely light.

Get a mental picture of how you intend to be when your grandchildren are grown. This mental picturing helps program your destiny. Your body will be an old woman's body, but that is not a terrible thing. Japanese artist Manabu Yamanaka, who has photographed women of very advanced age, described them as beautiful, "like the last flickering of a candle." It seems that well after "pretty" ceases to be an issue, the beauty that accompanies wisdom and experience can come into its glory. See yourself at that time of life, proud of your accomplishments and at peace with yourself. Envision having good health, friends and admirers of all ages, and maybe a few regrets but not very many.

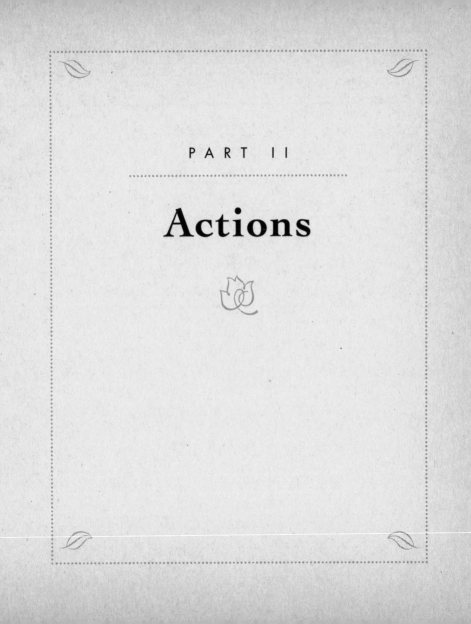

PART II

Actions

7

Adopt One Better Habit

Be proud of yourself for every incremental change.
These are the ones that will last.

Adopt one better habit. This is a gentle way to change. Note the word *better* instead of *good*. If you have a "bad" habit—being sedentary, for instance—and you want to develop a "good" one—for instance, running four times a week—the likelihood of a coach-potato-to-athlete transformation is pretty slim. You'll likely overdo, get injured, and quit, or you'll realize how hard running is for an out-of-shape person and you'll give up.

A "better" habit might be walking for half an hour on Saturday morning. It's not much, but it's better than no exercise at all. Don't even let yourself do more than that for the first few weeks. Then you can double up: walk on Saturdays and Tuesdays. After a month, add Thursdays. When you're an established walker—three months minimum—you can start running for part of your walking time once a week and build on that if you like.

This is not just a molasses-slow way to build new habit patterns; you'll actually be holding yourself back. As a result, you'll be chomping at the bit to make progress instead of going for too much too soon and ending up back where you started. If you played the game of "Mother May I" as a child, you can think of this as taking secure baby steps instead of a shaky giant step.

You can use the one-better-habit system in any area of your life. I realized long ago that drinking coffee was not good for me. In my body, caffeine is definitely a mood-altering chemical, to the point that I wasn't just drinking coffee, I was using it. Every time I went cold turkey on my java addiction, I'd be resolute for one week or several, until some lethargic afternoon when I gave in to the artificial energy boost I was missing. That's when I realized that I could cut down on caffeine—and maybe succeed this time—by going easier on myself and simply adopting a "better" habit. My plan: to drink tea—not green tea or herbal tea, just tea. I was partial to Earl Grey when I could get it and was satisfied with plain old whatever's-in-the-bag the rest of the time.

Is drinking tea every day a good habit? Maybe—there is some evidence of anticancer phytochemicals in black tea as well as green—and maybe not: it does stain my teeth, and even though drinking it doesn't make me jumpy or irritable like coffee did, there's definitely a little buzz. But it's *better*, for me anyway, than drinking coffee was. And the proof of the pudding is,

I no longer need coffee, I'm making my tea a bit weaker than I used to, and I sometimes opt for a well-blended herbal instead. This way, there's still some bounce in my step, but I'm not bouncing off any walls.

So, adopt one better habit: one *easy* better habit. Give yourself permission to do something else better later, one habit at a time. Be proud of yourself for every incremental change. These are the ones that will last.

8

Look Good Enough Every Day

Few women carry off sackcloth and ashes with much style.

Look good enough every day. This is not the same as the health class dictum, "Always look your best." Of course you won't always look your best. You look your best at your wedding or your daughter's wedding, for an important job interview or opening night at the opera. For going to the grocery store, you only have to look as good as you need to in order to forget about yourself and be absorbed in the business at hand—in this case, assessing the relative merits of peaches and nectarines or remembering paper towels even though they're not on the list. At times like this, you don't have to look great, just acceptable enough so that if you meet a business associate in the cereal aisle, you won't wish you hadn't.

The idea of looking good enough was presented to me as a biblical misquote from Dede, the woman who looked after me when I was a child. She regaled me with her mother's "old sayings" and was adept at paraphrasing scripture or Shakespeare so the point came out the way she wanted it. One of her restatements was, "God gave you a beautiful temple, and you're supposed to decorate it." It was a long time before I realized that wasn't verbatim. The New Testament passage is, "Know ye not that your body is a temple of the spirit? . . . Therefore, glorify God in your body and your spirit." A worthwhile sentiment came through Dede's version, though: take care of yourself. Look nice. Few women carry off sackcloth and ashes with much style.

At some point, however, that message was overridden in my mind by the more persistent one from the advertisers: "Buy our products and look good our way." I tried hard to do that, but it wasn't very satisfying—certainly not enough that I thought of getting ready in the morning as a way to "glorify God." Eventually I resented the time it took to fix myself up for public view. Of course, the very day I'd go out in ratty sweats and the face I woke up with, I'd run into someone who expected to see me looking pulled together. I'd feel embarrassed, make some excuse, and wonder why there was never a hole nearby when I needed to crawl into one.

It all seemed so unfair, anyway. Why couldn't I just go out looking how I happened to look? No reason, I finally figured out, as long as I felt good about it. But I didn't. Then I remembered Dede, and the temple. And that offering an agreeable physical presence to the world is not to support the fashion industry or to elicit the attention of men and the envy of other women. Its value lies in the fact that the highest and finest parts of us aren't visible on their own; we pay them homage by doing some basic "temple maintenance" before going out into the world, even if the world today consists only of the health club and the post office.

Since I know that I feel better when I look at least presentable and preferably polished, you'd think I'd look that way all the time. I don't. Sometimes I'm just too rushed or preoccupied with more pressing matters to bother with it. That's life. But at other times I simply *don't feel like having a good day*. Maybe I don't think I deserve it, or I don't want to expend the energy to prepare for one. But in pushing myself to do that a couple of times, I learned a precious little secret: if I make myself look as if I feel deserving and have energy, I find that I do. It is astonishing to me that not only can we alter our outward circumstances by changing our attitude, we can also alter our attitude by changing our circumstances. Or changing our clothes, when that's applicable.

As a woman becomes more content with herself, she feels less pressure to appear "perfect." At the same time, the habit of routinely looking respectable becomes the natural way of things. This is because it is an affirmation of life. I read about a woman who celebrated her 105th birthday, not in a nursing home, as the majority of centenarians seem to do, but at the newspaper office where she has worked as a proofreader since she was sixty-five. One of her tips for longevity was to always try to look nice. Of course. Then you're ready for anything.

9

Groom Yourself Impeccably

Just about anybody can be transformed in a bathroom.

W hen I was fifteen, I went to charm school. I can't think of a more outdated or politically incorrect place than that. We learned to sit "like ladies," walk with books on our heads, and be coy and coquettish. I had to unlearn a good deal of that stuff. Nevertheless, I'm glad I went, because charm school also taught "good grooming." It was sort of embarrassing, all the talk about blackheads and deodorant, but it did impress me with the unavoidable fact that just about anybody can be transformed in a bathroom.

The biggest difference between women who seem naturally attractive and those who don't is that the attractive ones are impeccably groomed almost all the time. They're adept at preventive maintenance. While most of us do our nails when we notice that the polish has chipped or touch up our roots when we see them in the mirror, the impeccably groomed take care of these details before they're visible. It's simply habit. It's also important to them. A little of this kind of attention, as long as it doesn't go to the extremes of vanity or self-absorption, is a way to respect yourself and the people you interact with, each one an expression of the divine. And if you believe in God, God sees you, too. That alone is worth washing your hair.

In the most fundamental sense, grooming is keeping clean. When we expand the definition, it becomes a combination of what you do to care for yourself daily and weekly and what you hire someone to do for you at other times. Both should be pleasant, and neither has to cost a lot. First, figure out how groomed you want to be. For instance, most American women wouldn't feel right without shaving or waxing their legs and underarms, but a few think it's silly, even oppressive. And in some other cultures, it simply isn't done.

Once you know what you want to do, do it without fail. If you find that you just don't have time to maintain yourself the way you want to, you may have made yourself too high maintenance for this stage of your life. For example, a teenager usually has a lot of time to spend preening herself. A young working woman probably has less time but more money. A new mom with a husband in school may not have much of either. Work with the stage you're at, and respect the inklings that come from inside you.

If you're feeling, for example, that you'd like to cut off most of your hair and become a wash-and-wear woman, pay attention. Maybe you need more time, and having less hair could be a way to get it; or perhaps you have more freedom now, and shorter hair is a way to show it. A friend of mine dispensed with some really fabulous, trademark dreadlocks when her son left for college. After spending nearly eighteen years as a single mother and successfully presenting the world with a bright, talented young man, she was ready to cut loose—and cut hair.

Other women have condensed their grooming routines by letting their hair be its natural color, by scrapping artificial nails and their constant upkeep, or by learning a three-minute make-up routine that is sufficient for most days. (Go to a department store where they're doing free demonstrations.) Some women, of course, dispense with makeup entirely and look just fine.

Choose products that are so enticing you actually look forward to using them. Some cosmetic lines, usually the most natural ones on the market, seem to forge a bond with certain individuals. This goes beyond their effectiveness to a sort of chemical attraction; it's almost like having a crush on your cleanser.

You also want to have a real meeting of the minds with the people who support you in your personal upkeep. The basics are having somebody who can cut hair and somebody who can clean teeth and seeing them on schedule. Beyond that, you may have a dermatologist, an esthetician (facial person), a massage therapist, a manicurist, and others you visit either frequently or on occasion. Either way, these helpful folks form a resource bank; they're there when you need them. The idea is to find people who will listen to you, who understand what you want, and who are skilled at what they do.

Ask for recommendations from people you trust. Find out what these various professionals charge; if one is out of your price range, there are plenty of others who are in it. Sometimes the fanciest salons and spas aren't the best anyway. And if the atmosphere is intimidating or the welcome cold, it defeats your underlying purpose of feeling splendid about being who you are. Remember, whether it's a physician or a nail tech, you're *hiring* this person; for half an hour anyway, they're your employee. You can respect their expertise, but they need to respect that you're paying their rent.

And although it's not specifically a grooming issue, add to your list of helpful people the rare man or woman who knows how to sew. Forty years ago, even midpriced department stores offered gratis tailoring on anything purchased. Those days are over, and we're made to feel that not being a perfect size what- ever is some dreadful flaw. Not so. The rich have their clothes altered, and the models in the magazines have theirs tucked and pinned. When you find someone who is gifted with a needle and thread, it frees you from the minor tyranny of "off the rack," and everything you own can look as if it were made for you.

The point of all this from a spiritual perspective is that you deserve to feel as confident about your outside self as your inside one. As spiritual beings, we accepted the limitations of physical form in exchange for its wonders. Some people take to this like ducks to water. They're comfortable in their bodies— and with them. Others are more at home in the realm of thought and feeling. For them, taking care of a body is a lot of work, and they often feel they're just not getting it. They can feel as if their radiant soul is trapped in a body that doesn't reveal what's inside. If that sounds like you, go easy on yourself. Think of the care you give your body as a way to liberate your spirit. God has created billions of bodies and loves all of them. For this moment, you only have to be concerned with one. Take good care.

10

Move Your Body

If someone is in a serious accident, our first question is, "Will he able to walk?" And yet most of us who can walk just fine do it as little as possible.

Young beings love to move about. Toddlers and puppies are experts at it. At some point, however, most of us take a liking to automobiles, elevators, and easy chairs. Whether we opt for indolence at five or fifty, our bodies suffer from lack of use and our souls from being attached to such a lethargic apparatus. I speak from experience. I stopped going out to play as an elective activity the first time I wasn't picked for a team—or maybe it was when some other little girl called me "fatty" on the playground. In any case, I cut out all that running and skipping stuff early on. I am not fond of sweating and panting to this day. If you're not either, I suggest that you stop looking at exercise as something you "should" do. That makes it too easy to skip a session when time is tight or to rationalize that an injury to one part of the body is ample reason for immobilizing the whole thing. Instead, arrange your life so that exercise is inevitable.

The experts used to think that exercise only counted if it was done in a chunk—running: twenty minutes; spinning class: thirty minutes, and so forth. They now see the error of their ways. It all counts. Activity adds up—five minutes here, ten there. Life itself, when we put some energy into it, takes care of us. The most natural way to become an active person is to walk where you're going. We regard the inability to walk as a tragedy. If someone is in a serious accident, our first question is, "Will he be able to walk?" And yet most of us who can walk just fine do it as little as possible.

I realize that walking is no longer a viable means of short-range transportation for many of us. The landscape is awash with parking lots; myriad subdivisions boast every amenity except sidewalks; and countless people, if they walk at all, have to do it on a treadmill. This is such a pity. The woman who walks a few miles in the course of her daily life tends to have great legs, bright eyes, and clear skin, especially if she walks outside. She is also likely to have a cheerful attitude from the endorphins circulating through her system and a hearty appetite she can satisfy with delicious food and no calculating of calories or fat grams.

If you can't walk everywhere, at least walk somewhere. Walk your kids to school. Walk with your dog in the park. Walk after lunch or after work or after dinner. Invite a friend to join you for a hike or a stroll. Use public transportation, and walk to the bus stop or the train station. Frequent neighborhood businesses, and walk to them. If there aren't any businesses in your area, is there some natural beauty nearby that makes you want to get out and walk? (I firmly believe that everyone deserves to live within walking distance of either beauty or convenience, if not both.) Find ways to make walking interesting. Maybe you appreciate architecture or birds or faces. Think of your walking environment as a moving gallery.

You can also use your body in both work and play much more than most people do by simply putting your mind to it. Get your own glass of water from the kitchen. "Lose" the remote. (I know, your husband would have a heart attack. Believe me, he's more likely to have one if he's remote addicted.) Climb stairs. One study found that people with second-floor apartments lived longer than their first-floor neighbors. Think of what might help you be more self-propelled. Maybe if you bought a shopping cart, you'd walk to the grocery store, or if you had a good-sized basket installed on your bike, you would ride it for doing errands.

And for fun, find some mobile pastimes that are as appealing as sedentary ones. I admit that this is tough for me; I like movies, plays, concerts, books, and conversation. Still, I can have a good time roller-skating (mostly forward, nothing fancy), rock climbing (easy wall, big handles), and even weight lifting— okay, the weights are really light, but I think of it as practice in being powerful. For that, I'll sweat.

Ask yourself what you really like to do that involves your muscles. If nothing comes to mind, what physical activities did you once like to do? If you loved swimming when you were in school, you would probably still like it now. Discover the joy of movement in some activity that resonates with your personality. If you're an extrovert, you'd probably feel at home at a gym or on a team or in a walking group. If you're a more solitary sort, you might prefer a mountain bike or a pair of running shoes and an answering machine that says, "I'm out." If you're artistic, move artistically through dancing or figure skating. If you have physical limitations, see if there are activities they don't interfere with or if you can modify what you've always had fun doing so you can keep on doing it. If you're in a situation of being unable to do physical exercise, exercise your soul all the more with interior pursuits like prayer and meditation.

It's also wonderful to involve your spiritual practice in your active life. You can do a moving meditation by walking mindfully, your eyes open, your steps in rhythm with your breathing, and your mind willing to receive peacefulness and insight. Yoga (chapter 15) is one physical activity with a spiritual basis; another is tai chi, a graceful combination of physical movement and mental focus that grew out of Taoist philosophy of ancient China.

You can also walk or run to benefit a cause you believe in. After her daughter Emily died of leukemia, my friend Terry decided to raise money for the Leukemia & Lymphoma Society by participating in the most rigorous athletic challenge open to laypeople, the Ironman triathlon. When she started training, Terry, forty-one and nursing her son Timothy, was unable to run a mile. She trained anyway, nine months in all. And she completed the

Ironman: swimming 2.4 miles, then cycling 112 miles, and running a full 26.2-mile marathon—all in under seventeen hours. "I
never felt once that I couldn't make it," she said. "I felt surrounded by angels all day long." Anyone who questions that the soul
can affect the body needs to talk to Terry.

In much more prosaic circumstances, any of us can involve
our inner selves at the tennis court or the jogging track by
remembering to be grateful. You might be grateful for the ability to walk or run. Or for how good it feels to put on a leotard
and be happy with yourself in it, either because your body is in
better shape than it used to be or because your attitude is. You
can say thank you for the wonderful sensations that come from
expending energy and going beyond what you thought you
could do.

Competitive sports can be at odds with spiritual practice
when they pit one person against another in militaristic fashion,
but you can put some soul into those, too, if you get pleasure
from them. Just play with all that's in you and let the score be
what it will, or compete like crazy for the duration of the game
and let it go as soon as it's over. This is what spiritual teachers
refer to as nonattachment. With it, you can feast on life's
delights and not be a slave to any of them, including coming in
first.

Martha Graham said of dance, "One becomes an athlete of
God." What a lovely thought. It flies in the face of the misguid-
ed philosophy that the body and soul are on opposite sides and
that Providence has a decided preference for the latter. Surely it's
preferable to be an athlete of God. This doesn't require becom-

ing a professional dancer or having extraordinary physical gifts. It can mean flying a kite with some child in your life and being thrilled about it, or riding your stationary bicycle in the morning before anyone else is up and knowing with all that's in you that you are not alone.

11

Take a Saturday Night Bath

*A Saturday night bath requires an hour. The senses
involved in it should, ideally, be all five.*

Showers are refreshing and invigorating. They save time and
water. But if you've ever questioned whether or not you're
worth indulging, a long, luxurious bath should convince you
that you are. Besides, cleanliness *is* next to godliness. Lowell
Fillmore, a pioneer of the Unity movement, stated it well: "You
have the great responsibility of keeping [your body] in order,
clean, pure, beautiful, and holy."

There's something else, too: when you bathe, you have to
take your clothes off. So many women despise their bodies and
live from the neck up, ignoring the rest of themselves as best
they can. In order to take a bath, you can't help but acknowledge that your body is there. When it's being caressed by the

heavenly warmth, you and your body share the pleasure. Your tummy needs to feel the massage of the water, whether or not you think it's flat enough. Your hips, your thighs, your breasts, and all other parts of you deserve this attention as well.

We often bear unconscious animosity toward certain parts of our bodies for not living up to expectations (ours or the media's), so we ignore those parts and deny them pleasure. We might even say to a lover, "Don't touch me there," *there* being wherever we think we're too large, too small, too flabby, too fleshy, too bony, or imperfect in some other way. In the bath, we can make peace with these neglected parts. Think of yours as an equal opportunity bathtub; an unsatisfactory abdomen gets the same loving care as an acceptable ankle.

To this end, I suggest reviving the tradition of the Saturday night bath. Before running water was common in rural America, country dwellers knew well the Saturday night bath that would make everyone presentable for church on Sunday. We need a version of this custom nowadays because we're so busy that a quick shower or cursory dip is all we usually get. We owe ourselves the weekend extravagance of a really special bath.

What separates a Saturday night bath, regardless of what day you enjoy it, from a Monday-morning-get-me-out-of-here bath are time, intention, and level of sensory involvement. A Saturday night bath requires an hour. Your intention in taking one is more to have an experience than to just get clean (although it does that, too). The senses involved should, ideally, be all five.

Devise the kind of Saturday night bath that will make you feel relaxed and pampered. If you like the idea of a candlelight

bath, keep matches and candles with adequate wicks in the
bathroom so they'll be handy. A bath pillow helps a lot if your
tub doesn't comfortably fit your back. If you want to listen to a
tape or CD, let your mood dictate your choice of music. Tonight
may be for Tchaikovsky or Gregorian chants or Judy Garland.
Provide yourself with a fresh bath mat and a couple of soft,
thick towels. Pour a glass of water with lemon wedges and have
some grapes or strawberries to munch while you're in the tub.

Run the bathwater almost hot but not quite; French women
swear that bathing in very hot water causes the breasts to sag
prematurely. While the tub is filling, cleanse your face and put
on a good dose of moisturizer; the warmth from the tub will
help it work. Then give all your skin except that on your face a
dry skin brushing. You can find brushes for this purpose at natural food stores and upscale pharmacies. With you and the
brush both dry, brush your entire body using circular motions.
This stimulates circulation and helps the skin, the body's largest
organ, do its job of eliminating toxins.

When your tub is full, transform it into a healing spa with a
few drops of pure, essential oil. Choose the one you prefer, and
mix three to five drops of it with one tablespoon of mild vegetable oil. (To be used safely and effectively in your bath, essential oils must be "carried" by a neutral oil like almond or
sunflower, not used alone.) Add the blended oils to your bath
after you turn off the water.

Aromatherapy philosophy suggests that each essential oil
has its own effects on the body and mind. For instance, to
increase detoxification when you're fasting or if you've been

feeling sluggish, try oil of rosemary or everlasting. To put you in the mood for romance, consider oil of sandalwood or clary sage. If you're fighting a cold, use eucalyptus or cypress. Laurel and juniper are classics for stiff muscles and sore joints.

Match the mood, and the scent if you like, with the soap, shampoo, and conditioner you choose. Many products add some extract of a flower or herb and claim to be "natural," but relatively few brands are strictly so. Since you absorb some of every product your put on your skin or your scalp, shop as carefully for these as you do for the food you eat. Explore the body care department at a well-stocked natural food store. Test different brands at day spas and department stores. Read labels. Open bottles and sniff. When you find products that really suit you, you'll look forward to using them. At the very least, use the mildest products that will do the job. Harsh soaps strip your skin of its protective acid mantle. You don't need "deodorant soap." You're taking a bath, for heaven's sake; you'll come out smelling just fine.

Take your time. Listen to the music. Focus on the scent you've chosen and where you want it to take you. You can work a little—sloughing rough skin with a loofah maybe—but for the most part, relax. Think lovely thoughts. Let yourself feel good all over. If you're not going out, save washing your hair for the morning so you can go straight to bed without the roar of a blow-dryer between a relaxed you and relaxing sleep. Emerge slowly from your bath. While your skin is still damp, massage in a natural body lotion; then dry off with one of those wonderful towels.

And take this seriously. So much has been said about the relaxing, rejuvenating properties of a long, warm bath that it can seem like too generic a suggestion to be really useful. It's even easy to get cynical: "Yeah, right—take a bath and wash all your problems away." But the reason we so often hear about the wonders of bathing is that it *can* work wonders. This isn't magic, but it is awfully good therapy and you can't beat the price.

Give yourself a bath to write home about at least once a week. Block out the time as if it were an appointment with someone important. It is.

12

Get Your Beauty Sleep

*If your vitality is not where you'd like it,
reconsider the hours you keep.*

Weariness can make you look awful and feel worse. The ancient Indian healing system of Ayurveda suggests regular hours, a sensible schedule. This is seldom welcome news in a culture sustained by caffeine and adrenaline, but the inner light shines brightest through a body that is fully alive. That aliveness depends in large measure on your being in sync with nature: with the sun and the moon and the seasons. You can start by getting to bed at ten and getting up at six-thirty—or some reasonable variation. It sounds boring? Ah, there's the rub: we like the stimulation of pushing ourselves hard and overstepping our limits. But the limits are there for a reason. Our part is to understand and respect them.

When you sleep, your body detoxifies and repairs. You accumulate energy instead of depleting it. Not getting enough sleep can make you irritable and impatient, not to mention inefficient. It can cause dark circles under your eyes and present you with one of those days when people who don't seem to like you very much anyway to get to say, "You look tired," with feigned sympathy.

In spite of the importance of sleep, we've all heard people boast, "I was up till three, but I was in the office at eight just like always." Depriving ourselves of sleep seems to be one way we can abuse our bodies and pretend it's virtuous. This is a foolish deception. Sleep needs do differ from one person to another, and some people do fine on a little. The latest research suggests, however, that the majority of us need more, not less, than the traditional eight hours to function optimally. Times of stress increase our sleep needs even more. Generally speaking, anyone who depends on an alarm clock to wake up is sleep deprived. When a body has had all the sleep it needs, it stops sleeping. Simple as that.

Sleeping well makes waking up a pleasure. Start by eliminating the adversaries of restful sleep. In an ideal world, bedrooms wouldn't have televisions. Or computers. Or exercise equipment. These belong to the activity phase of life, and their presence invites activity. Either move such stimulators out of your bedroom, or camouflage them. The television might go in an armoire, your desk or treadmill behind a screen. Allow your whole bedroom to suggest relaxation. Choose bedding made from soft, organic cotton. It's pricey, so you may have to build a set one piece at a time, but once you've slept between sheets that contain no chemical wrinkle retardants and that have no pesticides in their history, there's no going back. (Even without antiwrinkle coating, these don't need ironing if you take them out of the dryer promptly.)

Choose window shades that block outside light. Darkness tells the brain that it's time for sleep. Treat yourself to artwork that is either sensuous or calming. And the next time you paint, select a warm, restful color. You might want to follow the lead of my friend Liz and add an ounce of essential oil to the paint. Any soothing or inspiring scent will do. Liz used a blend called "Joy" and believes that it helped draw her true love to her, since they met just a few days after she painted the bedroom.

Having such an environment can make you *want* to adopt Ayurvedic hours, in which the rising and setting of the sun have more to do with your waking and sleeping patterns than the fact that Edison invented the light bulb. Ayurvedic philosophy teaches that the day is composed of cycles with differing energies. The hours from six to ten in the evening are characterized by slowness and heaviness. If you get to bed by ten, this heavier energy helps you fall asleep and stay asleep. If you're up past ten-thirty, when a more stimulating energy predominates, you may get second wind but at the price of a good night's sleep.

Six in the morning is the best waking time in Ayurvedic thought because this is when the energy that supports alertness and activity peaks. You can sleep in until seven and still get these benefits, but after that you've lost them. I know that night people would argue this point. Still, if your vitality is not where you'd like it, reconsider the hours you keep.

Use a gentle alarm clock to get up until you've adjusted and can awaken on your own. My alarm clock has a lovely chime instead of a buzzer, so when I have to get up earlier than usual to catch a plane, I'm not jolted from sleep to waking. This transition is meant to be gentle and gradual. When it is, you'll benefit more from the sleep you enjoyed, and you'll more likely remember what you've dreamed.

If you sometimes have trouble falling asleep, following a bedtime ritual can help. Think about how you like to close out a day: checking the locks on the doors, lowering the blinds, looking in on snoozing children, performing your grooming routine, doing your spiritual practice. Go through each process slowly and quietly, recognizing that each one is bringing you closer to restful slumber.

Help yourself sleep by avoiding late-day caffeine (colas and black tea as well as coffee) and alcohol. A glass of wine can help you doze off, but you won't sleep as deeply as you would have without it, and you may not sleep through the night. Exercise early in the day so you won't have energizing endorphins—the feel-good chemicals from aerobic activity—pulsing through your system when you're trying to rest.

Some people swear by the soporific properties of drinking a glass of water and then placing a pinch of salt on the tongue. Chamomile tea is another mild sleep inducer. So is the aroma of lavender oil. Put three to five drops in a tablespoon of mild vegetable oil and add to a fully drawn, warm bath. Or just place a single drop of the essential oil at the edge of your pillow, and take its scent with you into your dreams.

13

Bring Your Body to the Silence

Meditation, or some similar focused discipline, is as
essential to spirituality as practice is to music or
patience to parenting.

The world is noisy. It's the squeaky wheel we're greasing all the time. In the silence, we open ourselves to something higher. That's why meditation, or some similar focused discipline, is as essential to spirituality as practice is to music or patience to parenting. And it brings out your inner beauty by inviting the spirit to be fully present in the body. Writer and performer Quentin Crisp put it beautifully when he said, "Align your body with the forces that flow through the universe." Your *body*. Of course the mind and soul get to come, too, but as the Zen Buddhists say, enlightenment is not some otherworldly state; you're supposed to feel it in your flesh and your bones.

With all due respect, I think of meditation as the baking soda of the inner life. Both define *multipurpose*. You can use baking soda to clean your teeth and clean the refrigerator, to absorb odors, relieve heartburn, and make muffins rise. Getting quiet and concentrating on what's inside is as versatile—and necessary—in your life as baking soda can be in your cupboard. For example:

Daily quiet calms your mind—while you're doing it and for hours afterward. You become a more composed human being. It takes a lot to get you ruffled. Your stress level lowers.

Meditation improves your health. Research involving people who practice the Transcendental Meditation technique has shown that they have hospitalization rates 56 percent lower than those of the population at large, 87 percent less cardiovascular disease, and 55 percent less cancer.

Regular meditation transfigures the place where you do it. If you meditate at home, your home will feel more peaceful. People will want to spend time there. Acrimony among family members will decrease, even if you are the only one who meditates.

During quiet time, you get in touch with your inner wisdom and your Higher Power. You can go on the Internet to get information; you go into the silence for creative ideas, intuitive glimmers, and divine intent.

Sitting every day develops self-discipline. This carries over into every aspect of your life. You'll be more consistent with exercise, more careful about your food choices, more diligent about your self-care.

Meditation cultivates qualities of soul: compassion, generosity, courage, and faith. This goes beyond improving yourself; it is rather becoming yourself, your true self in whom these characteristics are already fully operative.

There is something else, too. *Meditation makes you prettier.* Unless she is too modest to tell you the truth, any woman who has meditated regularly for a reasonable period of time will let you know that the practice softens lines, refines complexions, and imparts a radiance that wasn't there before.

My friend Lynda had been taking meditation classes every week and practicing at home daily for a year when she noticed that she looked better after class than she did before. Week after week, this slight but definite shift was apparent. Around the same time, people started commenting that she was looking younger, more rested—the things people say when they see us glow but don't know what to call it. Lynda finally concluded that the act of meditation confers heightened beauty upon the one who meditates. A little residual is left every time, and more and more inner beauty rises to the surface.

So take some time, preferably in the morning. Tradition suggests inserting your quiet time between bathing and breakfast. Sit with your spine reasonably straight, but be comfortable; you want your body to be an ally in this process. Shoot for twenty minutes in the silence; when you don't have twenty, ten will do. Regularity is important. Everybody misses a day every now and then, but meditating only intermittently teases your soul into thinking you're paying attention and then leaving it stranded.

You know what we say about men who treat women that way. Don't be a cad to your soul.

The simplest way to meditate is to simply follow your breath as it enters and leaves your nostrils. That's all there is to it. Your mind is likely to wander all over the place. When you find yourself thinking about the jacket you saw in a window or the grade your son got in math, gently bring your mind back to your breathing. Having thoughts during meditation is not wrong; in fact, bringing yourself back from random thoughts to focused breath is how you do it.

If you like, add related practices to your quiet time, framing the meditation as you would frame a picture. I pray first, before my feet touch the floor in the morning. I don't want to step into a day without first recognizing the wonder of it. This is also when I remember people I know of who are having a difficult time and hold them in the light. When I come back from the shower, I prepare for meditation by writing in my journal. Writing is a way to acknowledge thoughts and concerns before turning from them for a time.

If your experience is like mine, you will have some meditations that are extraordinary. You'll be transported to a state of sublime peacefulness and return rested, refreshed, energized, and bursting with genius. Other times you won't feel anything. You'll wonder why you bothered. Bother anyway. Your day has 960 waking minutes. During ten or twenty or forty of them, bring your body to the light. Take some light into the world the rest of the time.

PART III

Body and Soul

14

Befriend Discipline

Discipline is where beauty and soulfulness meet.

Discipline is where beauty and soulfulness meet. Most women we regard as physically attractive are exceedingly disciplined when it comes to their exercise, food choices, and self-care. And anyone with soul beauty shining through is scrupulous about spiritual practice, ethical conduct, and maintaining an affirmative attitude.

Practical, self-imposed disciplines are like boot camp for a glorious life. They train us for doing what we need to do at the right time whether we want to or not. We all have different obligations and expectations of ourselves, but there are some basic disciplines for inner and outer beauty from which anyone could benefit. Here are a few:

Practice temperance. Temperance is refraining from what's harmful and being moderate with what isn't. It is the opposite of self-indulgence, and it benefits both body and soul. Just for practice, when you're out for lunch or a drink, order the small size. When you do, you may notice how uncomfortable the culture is with "small." You'll often see it called "tall" (as opposed to "grande") or "large" (that is, a step down from "jumbo").

Have quiet time every day. You may have to get up earlier than you're used to or get in a little earlier at night. Whatever it takes, get your spiritual silence every twenty-four hours at least. One of the most naturally beautiful women I know tells me this is her only beauty secret. "Meditation," she says, "sets up an action in the universe rather than a reaction in you. You don't have to do anything else."

Exercise regularly. You know that exercise cleanses tissues, builds stamina, and firms muscles. It's also extraordinary training for showing up for what's next, whether you're in the mood or out of it. Exercise is also the best illustrator of how discipline can transform something you dreaded into something exhilarating. You can come home from work too weary for anything but the couch and the sitcoms, go to the park or the gym anyway, and get energy that lasts all evening.

Wash your face. Whether you wash with soap and water or cleanse with lotion or cream, do it without fail. Women with exquisite complexions never go to bed with makeup on. Those who are in control of their lives don't either. Self-control is when your mind tells your body to wait a bit before getting what it wants. Taking three minutes to cleanse your face when you would far rather fall into bed is a way to exercise this capacity. (Some holistic skin care experts say that since the skin needs to breathe at night we should use moisturizer only during the day and not before bed. If you take this advice, you just saved two minutes.)

Brush and floss. Taking care of your teeth can make them pretty, keep them healthy, and even contribute to a heart attack prevention program. (The bacteria in dental plaque has been shown to adversely affect the heart; flossing cuts the risk.) Use natural toothpastes and tooth powders available at health food stores and specialty pharmacies; they're tasty, effective, and chemical free. For fresher breath, clean your tongue in the morning, too. Use a spoon or a tongue scraper (in the toothbrush aisle at drugstores) to gently scrape the tongue once or twice.

Keep your environment orderly. If your uncles and in-laws are extended family, then your home, car, and office are your extended body. Take care of them as well as you do your body itself. You don't have to go overboard, but at least keep things picked up and cleared out enough so that you know where to find what you're looking for and so an unexpected guest doesn't throw you into a panic. One simple discipline is to follow the antigravity rule; that is, anything that doesn't belong on the floor doesn't go there. This alone should keep clothes, towels, and dishes where they belong.

Honor your commitments. We have major commitments, for example, "I had this baby; now I will raise him," and minor ones: "I'll keep this lunch date, return this favor, answer this letter." Honor all of them, unless following through on a lesser commitment would jeopardize a momentous one. If keeping up with your commitments seems to take up all your time, call a moratorium on new ones, and delete less important obligations as you're able.

Speak kindly or not at all. Silence is the greatest discipline and kindness the greatest gift. The challenge is to hold our tongue. Sometimes that's harder than reining in a team of wild horses. Get into the habit during times it's not so tough; then when you're dying to spread a tale or make a sarcastic comment, you'll be able to hold back.

Learn something. Make a point of finding answers to questions—your own and your children's. Look up words you don't know. Read. Ask questions. Take classes. Establish the discipline of learning something every day and then telling someone else what you learned; that will impress it on your memory.

Daily, find ways to serve. When I call my favorite yoga school, they answer with, "Integral Yoga Institute, how may I serve you?" I try to recall that spirit when I feel like saying, on the phone or otherwise, "What do you want this time?" The discipline comes in remembering that I am one servant among many. This is not to diminish self-worth: government officials all the way up to the president are called public servants. An attitude of service is not self-sacrifice to the point of exhaustion or resentment. Serve wisely so you'll have the resources available to serve more tomorrow.

"Do something every day that you don't want to do; this is the golden rule for acquiring the habit of doing your duty without pain." Mark Twain said it, and it's still true.

15

Explore Yoga

*Yoga can impart a degree of healthfulness to the body
that ordinary exercise, with all its benefits, simply
cannot accomplish.*

Yoga can give you greater access to your soul and more confidence about your body, and it can put bliss where anxiety
used to be. The word itself means union: with the divine, with
your true nature, with purest joy. Hatha yoga, which concentrates on the physical body, involves breathing practices, gentle
movements, and static postures to make you strong, flexible,
and balanced. In time, these become more than physical traits;
they carry over into a strong character, a flexible attitude, and a
balanced life.

When I came upon yoga at seventeen, it wasn't popular like
it is now. In fact, it was considered downright weird. Only a few
books were available on the subject. I remember that one was

called *Forever Young, Forever Beautiful.* Weird or not, that was what I wanted. The first benefit I received from the easy stretches, focused balancing, and quiet concentration of yoga class was that I realized what my body felt like. I had been living in my head to the exclusion of the rest of me. I didn't have to worry about my head's being overweight or ungraceful, so it seemed like a safer place to keep myself. Yoga carefully installed my consciousness below the neck as well as above it. The sensation was like moving from a cramped room to a spacious house: there was freedom to expand. When I was willing to own my body, it was willing to grow healthier and more supple.

Nowadays, yoga classes are easy to find, but don't necessarily settle for the first one you try. Some variations of yoga that are prevalent in the West today are not too different from the aerobics classes offered at any gym. Many are rugged and don't accommodate all kinds of bodies or all ages of practitioners. A studio might have bright lights to encourage competition with other students or mirrors to encourage competition with yourself. If this kind of environment inspires you, fine. If it doesn't, look for a class in traditional hatha yoga. You'll recognize it because the ambience is quiet and the emphasis is on turning inward. The pace is slow, and the level of fitness and flexibility you have right now is an ideal place to start.

Although the ancient sages who formulated the yoga practices were Hindu, yoga itself is not a religion. Anyone of any religion (or no religion) can practice it successfully. The spiritual component of hatha yoga is that it develops a body that is suited for communion with heaven and service on earth. It can also lead to a level of physical health that ordinary exercise, with all its benefits, simply cannot match. While conventional exercise concentrates on cardiovascular functioning and arms, legs, abs, and glutes, yoga also works on the glands that regulate all body functions. A yoga class may include exercises for forgotten parts of the body: the eyes, the fingers and toes, and, above all, the spine. It also features inverted postures that tone the endocrine system and increase blood flow to the head, improving the appearance of the skin and hair.

In addition, you might do some responsive chanting, believed to purify the body and mind; breathing exercises, which can increase oxygenation up to seven times what we normally experience; and meditation to quiet the mind and integrate the benefits of the practice. Following a yoga class, or after doing yoga at home, you are likely to feel joyous, regardless of the circumstances in your life; energized, even after a tiring day; relaxed, tranquil, and clear-headed. And if you ever doubted that your body, mind, and soul are a contiguous whole, each dependent upon the well-being of the others, you'll never doubt it again.

16

Purify the Instrument

*Fasting, in the right frame of mind and for the right reasons,
can make you glow like nothing short of falling in love.*

Nowhere has the mind-body connection been more obvious
than in the dual admonition, "Fast and pray." Almost
every religion has some version of this, although nowadays the
fasting is often greatly tempered to something like giving up
meat or sweets during Lent. The spirit of the teaching is there,
however: in doing without something, we make space in ourselves for more divinity, for more light.

Fasting also has a venerable tradition in terms of bodily
purification. Hippocrates wrote of its curative powers, and a
small but growing number of contemporary physicians use
some manner of fasting to allow the body a physiological rest
that enables it to heal. Many people who fast, even if they do it

for health reasons only, discover in the process a heightened spirituality. When someone is eating very little, or drinking only water in a complete fast, the sense of being sustained by a higher power can come through better than at any other time.

Fasting, in the right frame of mind and for the right reasons, can also make you glow like nothing short of falling in love. The theory is that, because digestion of food is an energy-intensive process, giving your digestive system a rest enables the self-healing capabilities of your body to go into overdrive. The body cleans house, releasing impurities at an accelerated rate. The result is sparkling eyes, flawless skin, and a youthful radiance. (And, yes, you do lose weight, but it's mostly water and will return when you start eating again. Fasting is about purification, *not* getting thin.)

Years ago, I spent the week between Christmas and New Year's on a seven-day fast with 125 other people in the gymnasium of the Ebenezer Baptist Church in Atlanta, the church where Dr. Martin Luther King was once pastor. We had come from all parts of the country to spend the holiday week without food, hoping to draw attention to world hunger. We fasted on water only, although the doctor in charge put a tablespoon of molasses and a tablespoon of lemon in every gallon of water to make it more palatable so we would drink enough.

The first two days, we were hungry. The next three days we were weak. But by New Year's Eve, most of us found our energy returning and with it extraordinary mental clarity, creative ideas, and a beauty we hadn't brought with us. I would pass other women going in and out of the washroom, and we'd smile at each other in the almost embarrassed recognition that we both knew we were sparkling.

No one should fast for a week on water without competent medical supervision, and no one who is under a doctor's care or on regular medication should attempt any fasting without the express knowledge and consent of her physician. There are a few conditions (diabetes, hypoglycemia, anemia, and anorexia among them) in which fasting could be very dangerous. Even for a healthy person, complete fasting (water only) can cause such rapid detoxification that doing a short, modified fast or cleansing diet usually makes more sense. The purification happens more slowly than with water fasting, so you can feel good through the process and you don't have to stay in bed. I like to do a modified fast four times a year, at the change of seasons, so I enter each new phase feeling strong and connected.

Some modified fasts:

The fruits-of-summer fast. Susan Smith Jones, author of *Choose to Live Peacefully,* gave me this program: Day 1. Cantaloupe; it's comforting for the first day of a modified fast, and it has a cleansing effect. Day 2. Watermelon, good for the liver and kidneys. Day 3. Papaya and mango, to tone the digestive system.

The three-day apple diet. Eat only red-skinned apples, all you care for, for three days. (When the noted psychic Edgar Cayce recommended this one, he advised taking a tablespoon of olive oil at the end of the third day.)

The weekend juicery. Start on Friday and go through the weekend drinking only freshly extracted juices. Vegetable juices may be drunk straight; fruit juices should be diluted by half with pure water. Keep your juice intake to two quarts a day or less.

On any of these partial fasts, you may also drink herbal tea (a steaming cup of licorice tea is wonderful during fasting). And, drink water liberally through the day. At the end of the fasting period, add heavier foods slowly. The first day or two, stick with simple fare like fruits, salads, and steamed vegetables. By the third day, you can resume your regular diet. If you've been wanting to improve your eating habits, this is a great time to do it since your tastes will be refined after your brief fast and you'll actually be craving fresh, healthy food. Keep up the work your fast began by eating more fresh fruits and vegetables and drinking one or two glasses of fresh juice every day. With all the vitamins, minerals, enzymes, and phytochemicals in raw juice, the fountain of youth may flow from the spout of a juicer.

Plan your fasting time so that, for at least two of the three days, you can be home and get some time to yourself for the spiritual side of the process. You may want to unplug the phone and let the e-mail collect so you can focus on turning inward. Devote extra time to prayer, meditation, and journal writing. Read something inspirational, or listen to a book on tape. Refrain from heavy exercise, but enjoy walks in lovely surroundings and an easy session of yoga or tai chi. Take a nap, or lie down and rest in the afternoons. Make this a time out from hurry and commitments. On Monday when everyone tells you how rested you look, you can tell them you got away for the weekend, because you really did.

17

Help Your Form to Function

Envision yourself as a woman of regal bearing,
and treat yourself accordingly.

The point of being in a body at all is to be able to do things and feel things. Therefore, we need to be fully embodied, that is, aware of what is going on with us in a physical way. We also need to be as functional as possible in the bodies we've got. Architects say that form follows function. To an extent, this is true of our bodies as well. When we are functioning at a high level, or even as we aim to do so, the body strives to keep up. An obvious example of this is muscle development in exercise: the body is called upon to do a little more than it can in its present state, so it builds what it needs to meet the challenge. We can also help our form to function by (1) maintaining proper posture and (2) availing ourselves of massage.

When you have good posture, your organs function better, your clothes fit better, and you look more confident and self-possessed. Still, *posture* is a fuddy-duddy word. It brings to mind the stiff bearing of a military recruit who looks as if his spine would crack before it would bend. Think instead of the word *graceful*. Who do you see? A ballerina? A village woman walking with a jug of water atop her head? A child who hasn't yet sat at a desk and who moves with joy in the place where effort has yet to settle? The dancer moves the way she was trained. The village woman moves the way she has seen other women move all her life. The child moves the way a person does before convention intervenes. These postural role models don't have a corner on the market, though. Anyone can move with this fluency. The way you stand, sit, and walk is an outer expression of your inner state. It's not a matter of "Stand up, shoulders back, tummy in" but rather "Walk proudly, breathe fully, and remember who you are."

More of this will happen unconsciously as a result of believing in yourself than consciously as a result of forcing yourself to stand straighter. Instead, improve your carriage from the inside out. Envision yourself as a woman of regal bearing, and treat yourself accordingly. Create an affirmation for yourself about being graceful, moving with fluidity and elegance.

When you notice your body sagging, allow it to gently readjust itself by remembering that you are a person of stature. Don't criticize yourself; just let your body lift a bit, as gently as you would lift a child from a place where she'd gotten herself stuck. Think of yourself as connected to heaven by a golden cord that attaches at the top of your head. Instead of thrusting yourself forward, allow yourself to "hang" from this cord. The very thought of it will put your head, neck, and shoulders in a nice alignment. It will draw up your chest so it doesn't cave in. That would round your shoulders down, making you look tired and timid.

If you practice yoga (see chapter 15) or other slow stretching movements, understand that these release tension from the muscles, allowing for a more organic and fluid way of moving through space. For this muscular release to have a lasting effect, you need to rest a little after each stretch. In yoga, the position of deep relaxation has a name, *savasana,* and it is as revered a pose as any of the others. To do *savasana,* lie on your back with your feet shoulder-width apart and your hands at your sides, far enough from your body that they're completely comfortable. Close your eyes. Let your head fall to one side so your neck isn't rigid. Breathe naturally. Allow yourself to completely relax, even for a minute or two. If you like, visualize yourself moving naturally and beautifully. This process sets into place what you began with your stretching. It takes time, which can be hard to give ourselves, but the rewards are ample.

Another way you can give yourself time, healing, and relaxation, and concurrently reopen any partially closed communication channels between mind and body, is through massage. It's hard to believe that something this pleasurable is serious preventive medicine. Believe it. Therapeutic massage boosts immunity, makes joints more flexible, improves circulation, and relieves stress so effectively that some enlightened insurance companies offer policies that cover it. Massage also helps you accept your body as it is now. It's yours. It's good.

If you've had massage but it's been awhile, get in for one as soon as you can. The immune benefits are said to last for twenty-one days. If you've never had this pleasure, look for a licensed massage therapist in private practice, in a medical or chiropractic office, or at a salon or day spa. The most readily available form is Swedish massage. This is the place to start; it will relax your muscles and your mind and leave you feeling good all over. Other somatic therapies include acupressure or shiatsu, in which pressure is applied to specific points to release pent-up tension. Reflexology is a treatment on the feet, and sometimes the hands, in which particular points are stimulated; these points are believed to correspond with the body's various organs, which may benefit as a result. Manual lymphatic drainage is a delicate surface manipulation of the skin to assist the lymphatic system, which has no pump of its own, to remove toxins from the body.

Choose from what is available and what you can afford. Try a different therapist from time to time. A massage practitioner I trust tells all her clients to go elsewhere every now and then so they can be sure they're getting everything they need. A bonus of regular massage is that it enables anyone who gets lost in her intellect, her job, or her family to come down to earth and inhabit her body. It's a great place to be present in the present, to experience healing touch, and to reward your form for its diligent functioning.

18

Speak with Your True Voice

*Your voice is, at any given moment,
a direct reflection of the state of your life.*

It took me a long time to make peace with my voice. Like so many women, I felt that I sounded high pitched and childish. The only time I liked my voicemail message was if I recorded it when I had a cold. So I enrolled for vocal coaching. "I want to sound like Lauren Bacall," I informed the instructor, expecting him to respond with something about airways and diaphragms. Instead he asked a question: "What is it about Lauren Bacall that you feel is lacking in you?" With no time to come up with an answer more clever than the unvarnished truth, I blurted out, "She sounds like she knows who she is."

Given this revelation, my instructor wisely suggested that we first ascertain what my true voice was supposed to sound like. If we didn't like it, we could always go for Lauren. I was willing. Willingness is the state you're in when you don't want to do something but you won't fight it, either. Dealing with the voice can take a lot of it, because our voices make us visible and therefore vulnerable in another dimension, the dimension of sound.

In addition, speaking is how we connect with other people. As humans, we have a great desire to connect, but every time we open our mouths we risk being rejected, rebuffed, or misunderstood. That's why sounding like someone else, or like ourselves when we were younger, can be a protective device: those people aren't here, so they can't be hurt. A related tactic is to whisper, which dares others to hear us, or to shout, which forces them to. Another is to unnaturally force ourselves into a lower register—that's what I'd been trying to do—in response to the outmoded notion that masculine characteristics have more worth than feminine ones.

The alternative is to discover and use the true voice we were supplied with in order to express our true selves. The same motivation that can make us look as beautiful as our Creator intended can make us sound that beautiful, too. Voices are as diverse as people are, and listening to one that is unobstructed, uninhibited, free, and clear is a pleasure.

To tap your true voice, think first of what it's there for: to communicate what you know, what you feel, what you need, and what you've experienced. No one has ever lived the life you're living; this gives you so much to share. People who judge public speakers rate them in two areas, content and delivery. If you believe in your content (what you say), it enriches your delivery (how you say it).

Therefore, value your wisdom, your opinions, your needs, and your right to voice them. Paradoxically, a helpful technique for valuing your own words more is to use fewer of them. In other words, indulge in less small talk. When we talk all the time about nothing in particular, we forget that we really do have important things to say. For one week, then, if you're game, just talk less. Don't be rude or unfriendly, but for seven days refrain from initiating unnecessary conversation. Say what needs to be said without extra chatter. It's a glorious experience to spend a week knowing you haven't rambled or bored anybody or said anything you later wish you hadn't. You'll also have more vitality (talking takes energy), and you'll find that the less you talk, the more people listen.

As for the sound of your voice itself, realize that you probably sound a lot better than you think you do. If you have an extraordinary voice, you already know it since people comment on it, but if your voice is simply pleasant, you may not realize that it's nice at all. In fact, when you hear it on tape you may wish you could permanently erase the evidence. But unless you've been recorded in a professional studio with a soundproof booth and an array of high-priced, high-tech equipment, you have not heard your voice the way other people hear it. Judging your voice by how it sounds on a home tape recorder or answering machine is like judging your figure by how it looks in a cheap dress. It doesn't nearly do you justice.

Once you're convinced that you do have some raw material to work with, think of imbuing your voice with the characteristics that best express your true self, your inner light. Turn these into affirmations you can repeat until they become a part of you. Say these aloud since it is your voice you're working on. For example:

My voice is like a loving touch, soft and soothing.

My voice is like a still spring, deep and refreshing.

My voice is like a Steinway grand, rich and resonant.

Like every other aspect of your physiology, your voice believes what you say about it and strives to depict your conviction.

Deepening your breathing will also support your voice. Simply stated, speech is the merging of brain and breath, of having a thought and putting enough breath behind it to turn it into sound. Deep breathing as the yogis teach it involves sitting with a straight back and breathing slowly, allowing the muscles first of your belly, then your upper abdomen, and finally your chest to move, then exhaling with control in the opposite direction—chest, upper abdomen, belly. This is called "three-part breathing" because of the focus given these three parts of the body. Do this every day for two or three minutes. (Before meditation is a good time.) It will oxygenate your system and strengthen your lungs, helping establish the physical framework for producing your best voice.

In addition, loosen up and play with the sounds you can make. Sing, even if people have told you that you can't carry a tune. Do imitations. (My husband has been known to impersonate Elvis,

Richard Nixon, and Ross Perot on his answering machine.) When you read to your children, give the characters in the stories voices befitting heroes and villains, and do the animal sounds with great abandon. Sometimes the best thing you can do to get in touch with your strong, natural voice is let out a good *moo*.

Remember, too, that everything you do to care for your body and soul also positively affects your voice, which is, at any given moment, a direct reflection of the state of your life. You know how often we say (or hear) on the telephone, "You sound terrific," or "You sound terrible." Happiness, sadness, anger, fear, and excitement come through our voices, even when we try to mask them. This propensity of the voice to mirror life also enables a woman who exercises, gets massages, and feels at home in her body to gradually develop a stronger, more confident voice. And spiritual disciplines like meditation, dedicating your life, and being of service can also impart a warmth and richness to the way you sound. You'll hear your voice become more pleasing as your spirit gets more of your time. Finally, give your voice the honor of being a carrier of kindness. When it is expressing love, empathy, or sincere praise, it can't help but come out beautifully.

19

Avoid the Uglies

Certain things would make anybody ugly. . . . Some of
these we consume; others consume us.

Certain things would make anybody ugly—even Cleopatra, Lady Godiva, or Helen of Troy. Some of these we consume; others consume us. The major players are hard living, food porn, and inner eroders.

Hard living is excessive involvement in activities that damage the body and spirit. Smoking, for example, is slow suicide, killing your body while your soul works hard to infuse you with greater life. It also ruins your skin. Quitting is so important that it's worth failing a dozen times if that's what it takes to succeed.

Drinking in moderation adds pleasure to many people's lives, but drinking enough to diminish your clear awareness of the present moment works in opposition to the soul. (It's no beauty treatment, either, since alcohol dehydrates the skin, depletes the body of nutrients, and can exacerbate spider veins around the nose and cheeks.) If you drink, go easy and for the most part stick with wine—organic when you can get it.

Casual sex discounts the sanctity of the body—the same body that we want to be beautiful and reflect our inner light. This isn't prudishness; it's simply compassion and respect directed toward ourselves.

Food porn is the term coined by the Center for Science in the Public Interest for food that ought to come in a plain brown wrapper. X-rated edibles are manufactured combinations of refined sugar, refined flour, salt, saturated fat, hydrogenated oils, and chemical additives that the body has no way of understanding. These do damage in their own right, and they keep us from eating the fruits, vegetables, and other good foods that make us look and feel sensational. A simple way to cut down on food porn is to eat what I call a "still-life diet." If one of the great masters would have put whatever you're planning to eat in a still-life painting, it's probably good for you.

Inner eroders are expressions of ill will toward someone else that boomerang right back to the one who's holding them. Two of the more egregious are gossip and prejudice. Gossip turns the spoken word, a unique gift only humans have, into a weapon aimed at another person. It is a pernicious habit. A spiritual teacher once instructed a class I was in to spend two weeks refusing to discuss anyone who was not present. It was like being issued a gag order. What do you talk about when you can't talk about other people? You gravitate, I learned, toward ideas, issues, art, and aspirations.

After the detox period of not discussing other people at all, we were told we could add back into our conversation references to their good qualities, their accomplishments, and their general goings-on. After the period of abstinence, however, class members were acutely aware of how even compliments can turn catty in no time when the person in question is not in the room. For example: "Jane looked great today, didn't she? And it's so hard for some-one with her body type to look good in clothes." The lesson: let gossip stop before it gets to your lips, and be on guard any time you're talking about a third person. When in doubt, don't.

That next inner eroder, prejudice, means to prejudge. We do it all the time. Although prejudice is less tolerated than it used to be when it comes to race, religion, gender, and ethnicity, preju-dice in the form of instant judgments can be harmful, too. An instant judgment defines another person in a snap. It's seeing someone on the street or having a thirty-second conversation and presto!—they're in the pecking order: better than us or worse. When we make an instant judgment, we assume that we know some other person's age, income, educational level, status in the community, and general worthiness in relation to our own. Women do this a lot with other women. For example, we might think of someone *pretty* as above us, someone *gorgeous* as way above us, and someone who looks slovenly as beneath us.

When we're sizing up everybody else, we offer ourselves for the same kind of judgment. In addition, every time we place another person above us on our internal scale, we wear away at our self-image. And every time we place someone beneath us, we ever so slightly mar our own soul. Besides, because appearances are notoriously deceiving, instant judgments are often faulty and can make a fool out of the one having them.

Although I try to be aware of mine and stop them before they surface, I made a blooper not long ago. I wanted to buy my mother something special and had decided on a sterling silver picture frame—a little one but elegant nonetheless. The other customer at the glass case of picture frames was dressed in old sweats and her hair was messy. Before I knew it I had determined that she couldn't possibly afford anything she was looking at. Recognizing an instant judgment, I caught myself and mentally erased my unwarranted conclusion. At that moment, the sales associate addressed the woman by name and helped her select not one tiny frame like I was there to buy but nine large ones for more than $3,000.

A lot of our judging is both unconscious and instantaneous. Still, we can change our patterning by making a point of responding to everyone we see with a different instant judgment: *expression of the Divine,* just like me. If you do this over and over, despite occasional lapses like mine in the silver shop, it will start to crop up on its own. The more it does, the freer you'll be.

PART IV

Just for Fun

20

Dress like Yourself

I challenge you to keep only those clothes that have your name all over them.

We've been taught that we're supposed to look like the women in magazines, wear what's in style, and cut our hair to go with our face shape. How about looking, dressing, and coiffing ourselves in a way that goes with our soul shape?

I hadn't realized there was such a thing until the day I was invited to a private closeout of a vintage clothing business. Just being around all that history and craftsmanship gave me goose bumps. I was taken with the hand stitching, the intricate buttons, and the back detailing that made coats and dresses from the first half of the twentieth century look as lovely going as they did coming.

I selected a remarkably preserved dress from the 1930s. It was made of a wonderful crepe from a time before synthetic fabrics. Although the dress may have once been pink, it was now a delicate peach, and it closed with hooks and eyes on the side, beneath my left arm. Once those hooks were fastened and I stared at my reflection in the full-length mirror, I realized that I looked, absolutely and undeniably, like myself. It crossed my mind that this may have been the first time my true reflection, in clothes anyway, had ever looked back at me from a mirror.

This taught me that there is an imprint on my psyche regarding how I want to present myself to the world. I don't have to wear antique clothing all the time, but I do need to follow my inner leanings about what to wear. When I do this, instead of falling for what's supposed to be in fashion or the best buy on the markdown rack, I maintain more of my selfhood. My interior and exterior align.

As you make the daily decisions about what to put on, which shoes to pick, what jewelry to choose, base these on more than what fits, what's clean, and what goes together. Think instead, "How can I best express myself today?" When you shop for clothes, don't depend on the advice of a girlfriend or a salesclerk. What do *you* think? And if the first question that comes to mind is, "Does this make me look fat?" at least follow it up with, "Does this look like me?"

Think of the ramifications of your purchases. Where was this item made? Were the workers treated humanely and paid a living wage? What is it made of? It is important for your integrity to know where you stand on issues such as the wearing of fur and to keep to the principles you've set down for yourself. Beyond that, have fun with fabrics, trims, colors, and designs. You have to get dressed; you may as well have a good time doing it.

Clothes are fascinating in the way that they affect our mood. This shows up in a variety of unrelated situations. Studies show that students who wear uniforms can more readily focus on academics. And putting on something spandex is a near guarantee that you'll go to the gym. It follows that dressing in a way that makes you feel like yourself will help you be more yourself.

Don't worry about having a lot of clothes. Some of the world's best-dressed women have far fewer than you might expect, but each piece was carefully chosen. I challenge you to keep only those that have your name all over them.

Dressing like yourself is one small but powerful way to step into being more fully who you are. This means that if you've ever envied cover girls, movie stars, or your-sister-the-pretty-one, you can stop looking up to them as idols and start looking across at them as equals. We're only talking about clothes here, and their significance in the overall scope of the universe is pretty minor. Still, anything that helps you feel more at home in your body will help put you more in touch with your soul.

21

Give Yourself a Name That Suits You

We all deserve to be called what we want to be called.

It used to annoy me when people did something different with their names. I thought it was affected and egocentric, and sometimes I'd call them by their former name on purpose. That was before I took a stand for my own name and realized that we all deserve to be called what we want to be called. Sometimes this can change a whole personality and outlook.

Even as a little girl, I knew my real self was Victoria, not Vicki, but I couldn't shake the diminutive. At age thirty-four, I moved out of state and, meeting all new people, was able to start fresh as Victoria. This time it stuck. It was as if I had finally grown into my name, and once I did people no longer balked at spending four syllables of breath to talk to me. I still occasionally run into people from my former life who call me Vicki. It grates like chalk on a blackboard, not because there is anything wrong with the name but because it isn't mine.

Having had this experience saved me from maternal angst when my daughter did the same thing. Her dad and I had decided when I was pregnant that, whether we had a boy or girl, the baby's middle name would be Adair. His branch of the Morans had emigrated from the Irish village of Adare and named the county and town where they settled in northern Missouri after their home in Ireland. Their spelling was a little iffy, and Adare became Adair.

When our daughter was born, we chose Rachael as her first name because it seemed old-fashioned, innocent, and safe, as if it would protect her from the dangers of the world. But when Rachael Adair reached her teens, the Rachael simply didn't fit anymore. So she started calling herself Adair, relishing its uniqueness and its ties to her heritage. The transition was surprisingly easy, and the transformation was profound and immediate. At fifteen, she chose her name and became herself: confident, competent, and self-assured.

In some traditional cultures, young people are given new names as they enter adulthood. It is a highly symbolic way to leave childhood behind and take on the privileges and responsibilities of an adult. I am a firm believer, however, in being able to do at fifty whatever you may have missed at fifteen, including, if it strikes a chord with you, giving yourself a new name. Some people choose to divest themselves of a nickname or to take on a name with religious significance or one that has a strong call to the heart: the name of the grandmother you always wished you'd been named for, perhaps.

This renaming, whether you do it legally and completely or just within a circle of friends, often serves the purpose of filling in where you might be missing something. For my daughter's sixth birthday, a convincing fairy princess came to enchant the little girls with her wand, her wings, and an ample supply of glitter. One of the games she played with the children was to let them pick their magical name. Most girls selected romantic names reminiscent of legends and fairy tales (Guinevere and Esmerelda were both popular). One of the guests, however, made a different choice. This little girl was being raised in the Sikh religion of India, and her given name, Sat Darshan Kaur, was, for a first grader in Kansas City, exotic enough. The magical name she gave herself was Mary.

You may love the name you have, or, if you don't, you may feel that changing it is far more radical a step than you're willing to take. At least insist that people pronounce and spell your name properly, that they don't shorten it or alter it without your permission, and that they call you by your name instead of some diminutive like "young lady." You have a name. You deserve to be addressed by it.

And if some unmonikered aspect of yourself is still yearning for a name of its own, try getting it through your e-mail address. In spite of the general impersonality of cyberspace, it does afford us the opportunity to name ourselves anew. If you are considering signing up for e-mail or if you have occasion to change your screen name, think carefully about what you want it to be. Within the limitations of the number of characters allowed and what someone else hasn't taken already, you can give yourself a name that suits you. And you can take on some of its power.

22

Select a Symbol

Whatever symbol speaks to your soul, put representations
of it around you. Let these remind you that you can take on
the qualities of the symbol you've selected.

We are made of the same stuff as all of nature. As such, we can identify with other expressions of the Divine. Some of these speak to us at a deep and personal level. We can use this affinity to enrich our lives.

Certain Native American teachings call for totems, usually animals of various sorts, to symbolize characteristics that a person or a group of people wish to attain or strengthen. We can do something similar by adopting a symbol that represents who we believe ourselves to be or what we want to become. One of my friends chose the turtle as her totem after being confronted with turtle symbols three times in rapid succession. She meditated on the coincidence and concluded that she needed several qualities that a turtle has: the ability to stay safe and protected, to move slowly and not do anything hasty, and to carry a sense of home with her during her travels.

I wanted a totem for myself, but because I'm an intensely urban sort, the only wildlife I identified with were squirrels and pigeons, and they weren't delivering me any cosmic messages. Then one day in a little interior design shop, I saw some golden stars of papier-mâché. They were probably for Christmas and this was March, but I knew I was supposed to have them. I hung the stars in our breakfast room on the low beam that a feng shui consultant had said we needed to "raise" somehow.

The stars did seem to lift the beam, but in addition I felt strongly as soon as they were placed that one star was for me, one was for my husband, and the other was for our children: my daughter, William's daughter, and his two sons. To me at least, the stars represented our promise, our potential, and our true identity. Stars are a lot like people. There are millions of them, each a light unto itself, and more are being born all the time. There is no limit to how many stars there can be, celestial or human. I loved the symbolism, and I'd found my totem.

Look for yours. It might be an animal or bird, a flower or tree, one of the ancient elements—earth, wind, water, fire, metal—or a religious or spiritual personage. Whatever symbol speaks to your soul, put representations of it around you—a piece of jewelry, a candle, a photograph. Let these remind you that you can take on the qualities of the symbol you've selected.

Also, be attentive to the times your symbol shows up seemingly out of nowhere. When you forge a connection with a particular image, you form an alliance that becomes operative in your life. You might see your symbol in a shop window, as a picture in a book, even on a stranger's T-shirt. Sometimes just spotting it can help clarify a problem you're dealing with or a decision you need to make. It is, in any case, a lovely affirmation that there is support all around you—from the pigeons in the park to the stars in the sky.

23

Establish a Self-Care Fund

Do not underestimate the power of treating yourself to what you yourself believe is important.

We willingly spend money on the mortgage and the light bill, shower gifts and orthodontia. Why, then, can buying ourselves a pair of earrings sometimes be so hard? It's because many of us take the valid virtue of unselfishness and turn it into the far less justifiable state of martyrdom. If you've ever done this, establish a self-care fund: money earmarked for taking care of you. That way, you will never again have to surreptitiously toss a tube of face cream into your cart at the supermarket and pretend it's groceries.

Your self-care fund can provide for massages, haircuts, cosmetics, food supplements, exercise classes, counseling, a quiet retreat—whatever attends to your physical, emotional, or spiritual self. This money is to cover life-enhancing rather than life-sustaining purchases and experiences.

To come up with your self-care spending plan, decide what you need, bare bones, to provide minimum upkeep of the vehicle that carries your immortal soul around. Then decide what you would *like* to do for yourself if money and martyrdom didn't even come up. Somewhere between them, with deference to fiscal realities, of course, is what you'll want for your self-care fund. Base it on the money you have (debt is stressful) and on the woman you are. You may go in for pomp and circumstance or prefer clean simplicity. Either way, do not underestimate the power of treating yourself to what you yourself believe is important.

As a personal example: my face used to break out at the drop of a hat. I thought I'd tried everything, medical and cosmetic, when I happened onto a skin care regimen built around washing my face with black soap (mud from the sea, they said). That soap cost twenty-five dollars, and this was some twenty-five years ago. Six weeks after I starting using it, however, I had clear skin. Maybe it was the mud. Maybe my hormones altered and the timing was purely coincidental. Looking back, I believe that the determining factor was paying twenty-five dollars for a bar of soap. That was a bold action. It told my cells and my psyche that I was serious. They got serious, too.

I'm not advocating financial impropriety, and often the simplest, least expensive products are the best. Even so, spending a little more on yourself than you're used to spending can convince your mind and body that change is in the works.

Once you have your fund established and find out how nurturing it is to be able to treat yourself well on a regular basis, you may want a somewhat larger kitty than you started with. You can probably get it by funneling in money saved from the unhealthy habits you let go of. There is already a precedent for this: when governments need more revenue, they often raise taxes on tobacco or alcohol. When you stop smoking or eating chocolate every day, don't let all the money you save be swallowed up by the greedy mundane. Set aside a percentage of it to care for yourself.

Another way to boost your self-care fund is with windfalls—unexpected money or funds that you know are coming but that you haven't yet allocated for a specific purpose. Windfalls come in all sizes and from myriad sources: gifts, refunds, bonuses, earnings from a hobby or sideline business. Promise yourself that every time you get a windfall, you'll reserve a portion for taking care of yourself. One friend of mine developed a formula to follow every time she gets windfall. After subtracting taxes, she gives 10 percent to charity, puts 20 percent into savings, and spends 30 percent doing something special for herself. That way she's helped someone else, looked out for her future, nurtured herself, and has 40 percent of her net windfall left over.

You can also ask for nurturing gifts. When people ask, "What would you like for your birthday?" it's common to respond with, "You don't have to get me anything." But they're going to buy a present, or they wouldn't have asked. Help them not waste their money by telling them what you'd really love. Maybe it's a gift certificate to a bookstore or a day spa, a vanilla candle or lavender bath oil, an evening of baby-sitting or a dinner out. People want to give their friends what will really make them happy. Give the people in your life this opportunity.

Take Yourself Lingerie Shopping

A woman may dress well because she is secure or because she isn't. What's underneath tells the tale.

Shopping for lingerie may not count as spiritual practice. Nevertheless, having nice underthings is evidence that you treat yourself like someone who deserves the best, whether it shows or whether it doesn't. A woman may dress well because she is secure or because she isn't. What's underneath tells the tale.

I've heard that during the days of the Ziegfeld Follies, every new dancer on the line was given lovely French lingerie. This wasn't a strip show; the undergarments weren't to be displayed. But the young woman herself knew she was wearing them, and, so the story goes, that made all the difference—in her dancing, her demeanor, and her confidence level. We can give ourselves the same advantages, no benefactor required.

This is the drill:

Toss out anything torn, stained, or so stretched out it could no longer pass as a "foundation" garment. If you think it doesn't matter because nobody sees it, the implication is that you're nobody and your true love is nobody, too.

Arrange what's left in an orderly fashion. Some of us are naturally organized, and some of us aren't. Nevertheless, this is one place where even the creatively disordered might wish to take a different approach. This stuff isn't called "intimate apparel" for nothing. These are your very personal possessions; if anything you own warrants being kept nicely folded and categorized by color and type, unmentionables have to qualify.

Supplement what you have with some nice, new undies and sleepwear that make you feel stunning. Until you're well stocked on what you really like, shop to fulfill your own fantasies, not your husband's. If you feel beautiful to yourself, you'll look beautiful to him.

You may find a pleasant surprise in the lingerie department, too. Sufficient familiarity with what's there means that a voluptuous woman can wear a backless sheath, and a small-breasted woman can have cleavage without saline or silicone. There are undies without seams or fasteners so you can feel sleek and forget about it. There is sleepwear in soft cotton so your skin can breathe and your body can more easily do its nightly job of detoxification.

By regarding lingerie shopping as a combination fact-finding expedition and indulgent time-out, it becomes a way to have fun being female. If you're not the frilly type, lingerie shopping may seem more utilitarian than recreational. Try to have fun with it anyway. And whatever your type, remind yourself before you get to the triple-mirrored fitting room that you are beautiful exactly as you are.

Allocate a portion of your self-care fund for regular replacement of less than pristine undies, and note on your calendar every few months or so, "Shop for lingerie." Allow it to be a metaphor for more significant matters. If you're taking care of what goes on under your clothes, you're more likely to take care of what's going on under the surface.

25

Develop Your Sense of Style

You don't have to be rich, tall, skinny, photogenic,
or a graduate of design school in order to have style.
You have it now, and you can develop it further.

Style has nothing to do with spirituality but much to do with spirit—spirit in the nonreligious sense of your liveliness, your joie de vivre. French writer Marcel Proust sang its praises when he wrote, "Human words are in touch with the soul but do not express it, which is what style does."

Unfortunately, we've come to regard style like membership in an exclusive club: you're either in or you're out. But style only *seems* intimidating because people who have it can look so extraordinary we assume they've been given an aptitude we don't have. It's not true: they've only developed the propensity that each one of us has to express ourselves through our appearance, our surroundings, and the various graces we believe are important enough to acquire.

When I spoke to artists, writers, and marketing people at the corporate headquarters of Hallmark Cards, I had a wonderful time looking out on a widely diverse but consistently attractive audience. Some had a style that was trendy, some avant garde, others classic and elegant, but all of them seemed to regard coming to work as both an opportunity to create something and a chance to express themselves creatively. As one young woman explained it, "When you spend a lot of time in this atmosphere, everything in your life becomes art."

Any one of us can turn our lives into art. Here are some ways to get started:

Bury the myth that style is only for a select few. You don't have to be rich, tall, skinny, photogenic, or a graduate of design school in order to have style. You have it now, and you can develop it further.

Observe style. It comes in all ages, sizes, and income levels. Look for it when you people-watch, when you leaf through magazines, when you visit art museums and friends' houses. The idea is not to copy someone else's style but to get comfortable with the concept and come up with your own take on it.

Build on the areas in which your sense of style is already apparent. I can put clothes together because I've read fashion magazines since I was ten. For a long time, though, I was clueless about furnishing the places I lived. My friend Francesca, who had spent her allowance on *House Beautiful* back when I was spending mine on *Harper's Bazaar,* taught me how to apply what I already new about colors and fabrics in a different context. You can do that, too. Where does your style show? Think of your clothes, your jewelry, your house, the way you dress your children, the gifts you choose, how you set a table or garnish a dish. Take the flair you exhibit there and use it elsewhere, too.

Pick a base color. When it comes to dressing, black, brown, and navy are the most dependable base colors. If you stick for the most part with one of these for shoes, bags, and coats, you'll acquire greater style almost magically. It's a simple matter of time. Without a base color, few people have enough time to constantly change shoes, transfer the contents of purses, and track down hats, gloves, umbrellas, and the like that work well together. Once you have a base color, you can indulge in clothes and accessories that are as colorful as a box of crayons if you want to, but they'll be kept in check by your base instead of competing with one another. This way you'll always look pulled together.

Learn to tie a scarf. A well-placed scarf is synonymous with style, yet wearing one with panache is deceptively easy to learn. You can get an inexpensive booklet on it at a department store accessory department. There are dozens of ways to ties scarves, but knowing just two or three will usher you into the echelon of the stylish.

Have a few very good pieces. Whether it's a superbly tailored jacket, a supremely crafted handbag, your great-grandmother's cameo, or your graduation fountain pen, having one or two or three items of high quality bespeaks a cultivated sense of style. Everything doesn't have to be extraordinary, as long as something is. If you don't want to spend a lot of money, an exceptional knock-off may fill the bill; or look for the real thing at estate sales and consignment shops.

Know what you like. Pay attention to what you're drawn to in magazines, shop windows, art museums. You may even want to cut out pictures of clothing and anything else that catches your eye. Keep these clips in a file folder or manila envelope and look at them periodically. When you have enough of them, you'll start to see similarities. This is your taste, your style.

Incorporate your liabilities. I often wear chunky flat shoes or Mary Janes with wide straps and a buckle. Anyone who knows me would tell you that's just my style. And although there is much to be said for sensible footwear, in my case a botched bit of orthopedic surgery several years ago meant no more high heels, thin soles, or tapered toes for me. As a result, I've made the shoes I can wear integral to my "look." You can do this with a wide variety of handicaps. I've seen people incorporate everything from an eye patch to a cane to chemotherapy baldness into statements of personal style, as well as of courage and spirit. Make being petite, statuesque, or Rubenesque a positive part of your style. Accept yourself and any temporary or permanent limitations. Then apply your creative sense to what you have to work with.

Experiment. You're never too old to play dress-up. If you see something you love, try it on. It may be too expensive to buy, too formal for the way you live, or too daring to wear outside the fitting room, but take three minutes to feel wealthier, more elegant, or less inhibited than you are in your real life. When you push the limits, you find out where yours are. Your limits are fully acceptable, and they circumscribe your style.

Overall, developing your personal style is like taking tennis lessons: once you've done it, you have another game to play. The real secret, though, is to become a *style setter*. You do this by developing your gifts, your talents, and your character. Contrary to appearances, people desperately crave what is deep and solid. Give them that, and they will respond, gratefully asserting that the way you do things is the way they ought to be done.

You see this all the time in the volatile world of media and entertainment. Someone shows up who has average looks, but she gives an electrifying performance and a month later is on the cover of magazines. The world wants her gift; it only thinks it wants her face. So do what you can do well, and work to do it even better. Then you can set your own trends.

26

Play with Sounds, Stones, and Flowers

*These can be fun to explore with a sense of playfulness
and experimentation.*

To look and feel lovelier, healthier, and more at peace, you can do plenty that is tried and true: exercise and get fit; sleep and be rested; meditate and experience peace. Some other avenues to consider are less widely known and accepted. These can be fun to explore with a sense of playfulness and experimentation. The three I have in mind are sounds, stones, and flowers (or more specifically, flower essences). The efficacy of one or more of these may surprise you.

Sounds

I grew up on movie musicals and touring productions of Broadway shows. As a little girl, I thought that breaking into song on the street was a normal and widespread practice that simply hadn't caught on in Kansas City. We would all be better off if that childish conception had been correct and people did routinely sing in the rain and during other weather conditions.

Singing with a group of people creates camaraderie. Well-chosen music can also help houseplants grow, put babies to sleep, and cause people to feel romantic. Or energized. Or patriotic. Or reverent. In addition, according to Ayurveda, certain music can balance the body's energies, leading to greater health and beauty. The ragas of ancient India, available today on CD in the "world music" category, were specifically designed to attune the body and mind for greater serenity and effectiveness in daily life.

Chanting sacred sounds called *mantras* has a harmonizing and rejuvenating effect. The preeminent of these is the Sanskrit word *om*, regarded as the primordial sound, the Word that brought creation into existence. Intoning *om* can be at once both calming and empowering, and it is believed to increase *ojas*, or "healthy radiance," in the body. Another sound that can add to the beauty of face and body is *shreem*, said to strengthen feminine energy and encourage qualities of grace and loveliness. You can chant these sounds as a lead-in or closing to your meditation time, when you're doing household chores, or while putting your time in on the treadmill or stationary bike.

Similar benefits come from more familiar kinds of singing as well. You might consider joining a choir that's a fit for you both musically and spiritually—high church music from the Middle Ages, perhaps, or comforting hymns with familiar lyrics or exuberant gospel songs that could exhilarate anybody. Even music that has no religious connotation can fill your soul. I'm as elated by musical theater today as I was at ten. I know people who feel the same about opera. Any music that gives you deep pleasure or makes you gasp because it's so moving or so exquisite is the kind of music that will make you glow. Listening to it is good. Singing along is better.

Stones

Women who love jewelry know about the magic of something that sparkles and shines. I had never understood the allure of gems and stones—maybe because my mother adores jewelry and I figured she had enough for both of us. But once along the lakeshore in Wisconsin I picked up a small red rock, round and smooth and speckled, and brought it home. I've moved eight times since then, but that rock is on my desk today. For some reason I don't fully understand, I need it. I enjoy looking at it, holding it, and knowing it's there.

Perhaps because there is a rock on my desk that is somehow meaningful to me, I was not surprised to learn that Ayurveda has used stones in healing for over four thousand years. It is believed that they act on the life energy in the body, called *prana,* to increase vitality, longevity, and resistance to disease. According to custom, the diamond is particularly prized for bringing out inner beauty, but a stone you can pick at a rock shop for a dollar can have as positive an effect as a precious gem. Some stones and their alleged benefits include:

Aventurine—for courage, self-reliance, breaking free of convention;

Carnelian—for confidence and self-esteem;

Lapis lazuli—for deepening spirituality;

Moonstone—for decreasing stress and the symptoms of PMS;

Pearl—to impart a healthy balance of energy and calm; also for clearing the skin;

Rose quartz—for "rosy glow," increasing self-love, and attracting love and friendship;

Sapphire—for emotional stability and maintaining healthy weight.

People who use stones in these ways advise cleansing each stone that comes into your possession by covering it with sea salt for forty-eight hours. This is supposed to remove the vibrations of the previous owner and make the stone yours alone. This can sound far-fetched to those of us raised to think only in scientific terms, but truth comes in many guises. Besides, this can be play, remember.

Flower Essences

Dr. Edwin Bach, an English physician in the early part of the twentieth century, made his reputation by distilling floral extracts that his research convinced him had a positive impact on the mind and emotions. He formulated the Bach Flower Remedies to counteract what he believed were the underlying causes of human discontent, among them pride, unawareness, selfishness, and greed. The essences are designed to imbue the person who ingests them with the converse positive quality, thereby countering the negative influence and restoring health, which he defined as "total union between soul, mind, and body."

There are thirty-eight Bach Flower Remedies, each addressing a specific mental or emotional state, plus a blend called *Rescue Remedy* for acute fright or anxiety. There is *Beech* for intolerance, *Holly* to mitigate envy or jealousy, *Larch* to increase self-confidence, *Olive* for exhaustion or lack of vital energy, *Mimulus* for fear of known things (I know several formerly fearful flyers who credit Mimulus for their increased comfort in planes). In my experience, the Bach remedies do seem to ease the stresses of life, and, in situations in which I'm frustrated because there is nothing I can do, I can at least put two drops in a glass of water and drink it. It leaves me a bit more poised, a bit more centered, and as a result substantially more effective.

If you're interested in trying them, they're sold at natural food stores and homeopathic pharmacies. Spin-offs of these popular formulas may be fine, but I prefer to stick with the original Bach Flower Remedies produced according to the good doctor's explicit instructions. You can recognize them by their little brown bottles and simple beige labels. As in many aspects of life, there is something to be said for the real thing.

PART V

Quality of Life

27

Handle Small Things with Care

*Focus on one small thing at a time. This focus will bring
you the ability to tend to each one with facility and finesse.*

We don't stop at our heads and toes. The world also sees
the lives we create for ourselves through endless combinations of little things: the stamp on an envelope, the stationery,
our handwriting. When we dignify the small things, our lives as
a whole take on grace and beauty.

When something major is going on, we pay meticulous attention to details. Take a wedding, for instance. The bride, the groom,
her mother, his mother—everybody is hyperconcerned about the
invitations, the double envelopes, and that mysterious piece of tis-
sue paper that goes inside. The flowers, the greenery around the
flowers, and the baby's breath with the flowers all have to be
exquisite. Perfection is the standard for the cake, the punch, even

the Jordan almonds. It's no wonder the couple needs a vacation afterward. When you're cognizant of the small things in ordinary life, however, you're more likely to tend to extraordinary events with due diligence but stop short of obsessive scrupulosity.

My friend Suzanne is a master at this. She works with fine textiles, vintage and new. She has her regular fabrics, the big pieces. Then she has the outtakes, sections sufficient for trim or a hatband or to pass on to the ladies who make quilts. But Suzanne's heart always resonated with the tiny snips, pieces that seemed too insignificant to bother with yet were the last of something lovely she didn't want to lose. "One day," she told me, "I put them all in a bag and wrote on it: 'Scraps Too Small to Save.' But I saved them anyway, and I still do. When I use one on something I'm making, it's always the best part."

In our lives we have "scraps too small to save," particulars too minor to treat as anything but necessary tasks. And yet, like the treasures in Suzanne's scrap bag, these daily endeavors can be beautiful if we let them. This does not require mastering every domestic, social, artistic, and business skill in existence. Only Barbie can do all that, and she's plastic. Instead of aiming for impossible perfection, deal with each incident that presents itself. Focus on one small thing at a time. This focus will bring you the ability to tend to each one with facility and finesse.

When it comes to your appearance, the little things mean more than the big ones. People don't care about the size of your nose or the span of your waist, but unkempt nails and missing buttons jump out at them. Do preventive maintenance. Get a manicure, or give yourself one, once a week. It takes only twenty minutes. Every now and then, do your toes as well. If you wear makeup, don't expect it to last all day: perform routine first aid on fading lipstick and straying mascara. And unless you are committed to being entirely au naturel, get your eyebrows done every month or two; it opens up the eyes so remarkably your whole face seems more expressive.

Watch your wardrobe for loose hems, stray threads, little rips, and the like. Have pantyhose in your desk drawer in case you get a run. Look over your shoes every so often. Do they need to be polished or overhauled at the repair shop? In the classic movie *Sunset Boulevard,* it was noted that the shoeshine guy "never asked you about your finances; he'd just look at your heels and know the score."

In your life beyond your looks, handling small things with care is a similar process: being aware of what needs doing and responding to that need. In Buddhism, this is called *mindfulness,* making the business of the present moment your first priority. This means that if you're opening a birthday present, the ribbon you're untying is every bit as important as the gift in the box because at this instant, there is no gift; there is ribbon, and you're untying it. When you take a phone call, you give the person on the other end your complete attention; if you can't be fully present, you let the call go to voice mail. And when you pay your bills, you proceed methodically, one at a time, silently thanking the people at the cable company or the power and light for enriching your life and extending you credit.

These are tiny practices that, when you add them together, create a life that extends your inner light outward. Make a list of the small things in your life that you could treat with more mindfulness—and even a touch of virtuosity. For example:

When you send a note, put in a photograph or a bookmark or a pressed flower. (A businesswoman I know puts magnets with clever sayings on them in with invoices.)

When you work at your home computer, put music that you love in the CD *drive.*

Enclose something for the older sibling when you give a gift for a new baby.

When you give a presentation at work, use colored paper for the handouts, and package them in a lovely folder that participants can use again.

Put sachets in drawers and closets, and replace them every few months.

Write a note on a napkin for a child's lunch box, or hide a love letter in the suitcase when your sweetheart travels.

Light a candle for the heck of it—not just on the dining room table; on the kitchen table, too.

Instead of bearing the standard flowers or wine when you're invited to dinner, bring catnip or gourmet dog biscuits for the family pet. And put some of your own canine's favorite treats in a cookie jar. Your dog will know every time you open the lid that something good is about to happen.

28

Preserve and Protect

Protect your emotions from negative influences; protect your health every way you know how; and keep yourself safe.

W e safeguard our possessions as if each were a firstborn child. They're shielded by dead bolts and surge protectors, safe deposit boxes and insurance policies. We need to be as diligent about looking out for our own emotional well-being, physical health, and basic safety.

Protect Your Emotions from Negative Influences

Being informed is one thing; being deluged by all the pain and suffering on the planet is something else. I am devoted to the old-fashioned newspaper. A quality paper like the *New York Times* provides detailed information without sound effects and carnage in living color.

Use discernment when selecting your entertainment as well. Some people can see films that are violent, horrific, or simply depressing and leave them apparently unscathed. Other people can go to the same movie and not be back to normal for a week. I'm in their camp, and I've come up with a hypothesis to describe it that I call the "porous aura theory."

Some spiritual teachings assert that human beings—and, in fact, all living things—emanate an energy field around their body. This is called the *aura* and is supposedly what religious painters of the Middle Ages and Renaissance were depicting when they gave their holy subjects halos.

My theory is that some people's auras are tough, almost impenetrable. Others' are more permeable to ideas and influences from the outside. People with porous auras don't just watch movies; we absorb them. If you relate, exercise caution when choosing films, TV shows, and books. Avoid the ones that will ruin your day; they're not worth it. If you find yourself in a movie that you realize will make you miserable, leave. You're worth more than the price of a ticket.

Protect Your Health

Stop smoking, or never start. And avoid other people's smoke, too: at either end of the cigarette, this is nasty stuff. Projections are that at current rates a billion people will die from smoking this century. This is such a slight against life and its creator. Smoking also impairs the circulatory system, and you can give up on "rosy glow" without good circulation.

Get health care providers you trust. This isn't easy in situations where choice is minimal, but within the parameters of your health care system, be as choosy as you can. You want a doctor who will listen to your concerns and your opinions, who respects your intelligence as much as you respect hers, and who has expertise that goes beyond prescribing a drug for every minor complaint. If you get help from a doctor of chiropractic or a naturopathic doctor, these are "real doctors," too, with the same expertise in their fields that your M.D. has in his.

Use good sense in the sun. Life on earth, not to mention a lot of good moods, depends on the sun. Even so, skin damage is largely sun damage, so protect yourself. If you're fair, admire beautiful complexions of black and brown and olive. Call yours "ivory," and let it stay that way. Use sunblock every day, cloudy or bright. Choose one that protects from both UVA and UVB rays. Mineral barriers (look for the words *titanium dioxide, titanium oxide,* or *zinc oxide* on the label) tend to be gentler than chemical screens, and they're effective immediately—no twenty-minute wait before going out. Gloves and hats with brims help as well. Nineteenth-century women who had the means wouldn't leave the house without them, and that was before we had a hole in the ozone. (Two years ago, I had "age spots" on my hands. Now I wear gloves for driving, and they're virtually gone. Either I'm getting younger or it's the gloves.) Wear sunglasses, too, to protect your eyes and the delicate skin around them.

Support your bones. Osteoporosis, the brittle-bone disease that causes older women to appear stooped and can precipitate debilitating hip fractures, is preventable. You know about getting plenty of calcium every day, but are you doing it? Dairy products aren't the only source. Leafy greens such as collards, kale, and broccoli; almonds; sesame seeds; sea vegetables (like the nori that sushi comes wrapped in); fortified soy milk; and fortified orange juice are all calcium rich. Eating too much protein, especially from animal sources, weakens bones. Weight-bearing exercise (walking, running, dancing, weight lifting) strengthens them.

Keep Yourself Safe

Assess your safety status. How are the locks on your doors? When did you last test the batteries in your smoke alarms? Do you have a fire escape plan, and do you keep your car regularly maintained? In addition to tending to such obvious fundamentals, develop a protective attitude. You might visualize yourself surrounded by white light, representing the spiritual guardianship to which we all have access.

In a more down-to-earth way, the most powerful tool I know of for acquiring a protective attitude—and learning some potent skills in the process—is a good self-defense course. The most effective are those designed specifically for women. They have names like Model Mugging, En Garde, and Full Power. You'll be able to identify them because the classes involve enactments of actual attacks, with the students verbally or physically disarming an "assailant," a male instructor wearing a massive, padded suit and an NFL lineman's helmet. In these classes, you can learn and practice effective techniques for overcoming an attacker. This experiential approach programs the techniques into "muscle memory." Many women who have had to use these skills years after acquiring them have done so successfully.

I was hesitant about taking one of these courses, rationalizing that I was a peaceful person seriously committed to my spiritual life. Learning how to knock someone out seemed contradictory. I enrolled in the program anyway and mastered three priceless abilities:

1. *How to be more savvy and less frightened.* I used to be afraid of every man on the street who wasn't wearing a suit and tie. (Pretty poor criteria: serial killers often dress really well.) This certainly wasn't "spiritual," either, because I was sending vibrations of distrust to innocent people I could have been regarding with respect. Once I knew I had a good shot at defending myself if necessary, I could regard everyone who passed by with love instead of fear.

2. *How to fight.* My dad was a champion prizefighter as a young man, but I was never in so much as a schoolyard scuffle. I needed skills to defend myself. As women, we have strong legs, which well compensate for having less upper-body strength than men do. By attaining the proper competencies—not the least of which is knowing when to fight and when to wait—we can greatly improve our chances of surviving an attack.

3. *How to carry myself with confidence and use words to catch an antagonist off guard.* I no longer look like a victim, and I was once able to stop the beating of a woman on the street by simply shouting—okay, *screaming*—"Cut it out!" The man,

twice my size, was so shocked that he stopped striking the woman (his girlfriend, as it turned out) and was speechless: his mouth moved, but he couldn't make a sound.

We say that people who look good in later life are well preserved. So preserve yourself and protect yourself. Encourage your friends and your daughters to do the same.

29

Immerse Yourself in Beauty

Beauty rubs off. You cannot stand face-to-face with a
Rembrandt and walk away the same person.

We become what we look at, listen to, and involve our-selves in. A plain woman in elegant surroundings can appear elegant, too, as she takes on some of the ambience of the place. In Celtic mythology, that was the meaning of *glamour,* appropriating an essence of added beauty and allure—borrow-ing, in a sense, from the boundless beauty of nature and human creativity.

It is still our prerogative to immerse ourselves in beauty and let it become part of our bodies and souls. Any of us can wear something we love instead of something we tolerate. And if we end up wearing it a lot, we'll simply feel good more often. We can also immerse ourselves in the beauty of art and nature. By listening to glorious music, smelling delectable fragrances, and eating exquisite food, we grow more beautiful by osmosis.

At one time, I lived in London and had a volunteer job teaching "poise and grooming" to girls from low-income families in the city's East End. To my amazement, most of these girls had never been out of their neighborhood. The museums, theaters, and pageantry that define their city for a tourist may as well have been on the other side of the world. It was obvious to me that it would be pretty silly to teach "poise and grooming" to kids who didn't know what they were supposed to be poised for. So I changed the curriculum. Five days a week for a month, we took field trips. We saw paintings at the National Gallery and the costume collection at the Victoria and Albert. We watched the Horse Guard change at Buckingham Palace and the old guard shop at Harrod's. We smelled the flowers at Kew Gardens and heard the vespers at St. Martin's-in-the-Fields. I even negotiated a "day of beauty" at Elizabeth Arden in which each girl received one of the services. It wasn't that I thought these thirteen-year-olds really needed facials or pedicures, but I knew they needed to be treated royally in a lovely place.

Other than that day at the spa, neither poise nor grooming was ever mentioned. Even so, at the end of four weeks, the visible transformation in these girls was such that I felt like Henry Higgins—only younger, female, and American. Nothing had changed in my students' lives in any concrete way, but they had had experiences that hinted at the scope and wonder of the world. Their epiphany brought one for me: beauty rubs off. You cannot stand face-to-face with a Rembrandt and walk away the same person.

I believe that when you surround yourself with beauty, a change in your own energy patterns takes place. The new physics asserts that everything is energy and, as such, mutable. Therefore, we can change many of the underlying patterns upon which our lives and circumstances are built, and we can do so with surprising ease and speed. To accomplish this, we have to immerse ourselves in sights, sounds, smells, tastes, textures, and experiences that lift us up. In doing so, we create a personal world that gives us frequent infusions of beauty and delight.

Here are some ways to begin:

Make a date to meet a friend at an art museum or botanical garden. You can catch up on each other's news just as you would over lunch or coffee, but you'll be adding a dimension of beauty that will make the time you spend together special and memorable.

Starting today, purchase fresh flowers every week for your home or office. This guarantees one spot of beauty in your environment, no matter what else is going on. If a weekly bouquet seems extravagant, buy a single flower instead.

Make a list of things and places you consider beautiful and uplifting. Treat yourself to one of them today. Maybe you'll reserve a ticket to a concert or simply take a CD out of the case and play it. You could go to your favorite natural spot or simply drive wherever you're heading via your favorite natural route. Make a point every day to connect with something you've written down. And as your awareness of beauty grows, add more entries to your list.

Follow the advice of Goethe: "We ought to hear at least one little song every day, read a good poem, see a first-rate painting, and if possible speak a few sensible words."

When you commit to immersing yourself in beauty, you'll find your tastes either shifting slightly or expanding considerably. No matter how sophisticated you are at the outset, your world will enlarge. You will have an increased appreciation of beauty in all its forms, even the simplest. And because we tend to grow into what we focus on, it is not at all far-fetched to expect to see subtle changes in your appearance and attitude. Your life is changing. It only makes sense that it would show.

30

As Often as Possible, Do Something Thrilling

*If you put forth the effort to do something thrilling,
life itself will etch the joy somewhere that shows.*

It is impossible to be *over*-joyed, but strive for it anyway. Bliss works on both a physical and spiritual level to increase your beauty and enrich your life. When you are thrilled to pieces, your body produces chemicals that make you feel good all over. In addition, exhilaration leaves its imprint on the soul.

This is easier to understand when you think of its antithesis. When someone looks worn or haggard or just plain awful, we say that time hasn't treated him well, that life has taken its toll, or "What do you expect? She's had a hard time of it." No one would argue that trauma, grief, and worry can adversely affect appearance and demeanor. Jubilation has the opposite effect.

Sometimes, grand experiences just land in our lives for no apparent reason. (See chapter 49, "Be Ready for Light Times.") Doing something thrilling is different: it's you taking action. The first step is to practice saying yes to life. This is not the same as saying yes to overtime, baby-sitting, and serving on committees. It isn't crowding your calendar, martyring yourself, or neglecting your own commitments to please someone else. It is instead saying yes to opportunities for fascinating new experiences, even if they're outside your current comfort zone.

When my friend Nancy came over one summer afternoon, I asked if she'd like a glass of lemonade. "No thanks," she said, responding like the typical well-bred female. ("I don't want anything, I don't need anything, I'm not here.") But immediately she spoke again: "I changed my mind; I would like lemonade. Make that a yes." As I poured our drinks from the pitcher she explained, "I'm trying something different. For a month, I'm saying yes to every good thing that's offered me. Yesterday I even had whipped cream on a cappuccino."

At the end of the month, she reported feeling freer, more open to opportunity, and wiser about the world. (She also hadn't gained an ounce, whipped cream and all.) You may want to try Nancy's experiment. For thirty days, say yes to everything that sounds good and everything that sounds interesting, as long as it's safe, legal, and doesn't compromise your code of ethics. Don't let discomfort about trying something new stand in your way. Watch for phrases, silent or spoken, such as, "But I don't like the city/the country/the suburbs"; "I've never been a fan of country music/classical music/jazz";

or "That's too rugged for me/too rich for my blood/too far from a Holiday Inn."

Try instead a simple affirmative response, and seek to refrain from judging any experience until after you've had it. "Do you want to see this cool Iranian art film downtown?" Sure. "Do you want to go to my uncle's farm next weekend to pick apples?" Okay. "Do you want to meet our exchange student from Finland?" Of course. Not all these experiences will be in the thrilling category, but they'll at least put you out there where thrilling is possible.

As you expand your scope of potential elation inducers by saying yes to life, decide that every day you will give yourself one treat, bare minimum; you will indulge in some delight every week; and every month you'll do something that knocks your socks off. This gets you in practice so that every year or two or several, you can follow the advice of the Persian poet Rumi and "Start a huge, foolish project, like Noah. It makes absolutely no difference what people think of you." Ah—now *that's* living a life worth putting your mother through labor for.

If this exercise in ecstasy is to be effective, you have to know yourself. What do you like? What do you *really* like? What gets you a ticket to heaven and back? I get carried away by big, brash musicals and by any movie that can make me laugh, cry, or want to discuss it for hours. Learning new ideas and new twists on old ones is as exciting to me as riding a roller coaster—one with multiple loops. I feel elated when I give a talk and sense that I'm getting through to the people listening or when I've written something I know will touch readers because my editor put "Wonderful!" in the margin. And I am agog in the presence of people I admire and places where admirable people lived or worked or did something noteworthy.

When I'm willing to expend the energy to do these things, go these places, and have these experiences, I come back looking as if I've been to a spa. And in a way I have: doing something thrilling is like exercise and fresh air and healthy food for the soul. It lifts encumbrances and makes you beam.

It also buys you some regret insurance. Remember those people we spoke of earlier, the ones who could look a whole lot better? Chances are, the pain in their faces is less from what they've been through than from what they never did. People survive all sorts of dreadful things. Although some visibly carry the anguish for the rest of their lives, the others go on to have awe-inspiring experiences that sweeten the mix like honey sweetens tea. We are compensated for what we'd rather forget. If you put forth the effort to do something thrilling, life itself will etch the joy somewhere that shows.

31

Map Your Dream

The more your life reveals your dreams,
the more your face reveals your light.

We arrive on earth without an itinerary. Instead we have our dreams, our visions, to let us know what we came here to experience, accomplish, give, and do. The more your life reveals your dreams, the more your face reveals your light. You can amend a dream. You can alter it or even abbreviate it, but you can't disregard it without losing a piece of yourself in the process.

So that you can get busy on making your dreams come true, it is necessary to differentiate between a *dream,* a *want,* and a *fantasy.* A dream is persistent; a want is transient. Unlike a fantasy, however, the fulfillment of either one is possible. Let's say you want those sandals with the skinny straps that you saw at the mall. Maybe you get them and maybe you don't. In the long run, it doesn't matter much either way. Wants are the ultimate recyclables: this summer's strappy sandals become next winter's lace-up boots. Unfulfilled dreams, on the other hand, leave a gnawing emptiness. Your dream can be as big as you want—the bigger the better. It is, however, within the realm of possibility; otherwise it's a fantasy, that is, not achievable. "I want to own my own company" is a dream. "I want to be Queen of England" is a fantasy.

The fact that manifesting your dream is possible does not mean it will be easy. It may disrupt your life, strain your resources, and test your resolve, but cheer up: dreams used to get people beheaded or burned at the stake. The primary obstacle nowadays is fear. A reporter asked baseball great George Brett why, with so many good players in the game, there are so few stars. He answered, "Most players are afraid to be stars." Just like that, most people are afraid to bring their dreams into being because manifested dreams change lives. Change is the scariest thing there is—and the most inevitable. Convince yourself of this truth: your life is going to change anyway, if not in the direction of your dreams, then along some other course.

Once you're willing to go forward whether you're afraid or not, focus on the dream that clamors to be heard right now. Then plan its fulfillment by making a treasure map for yourself. A treasure map is simply a piece of poster board with pictures and words cut from magazines that suggest the embodiment of your dream. Hang your map where you will see it every day but out of view of anyone who would think it's silly. Look it over before and after your meditation time when your mind is

centered and your vision clear; and again before bed to impress
the image on your subconscious.

The average life span of my treasure maps is two years.
After that, so much of what was on them has come to pass that
there are new dreams to grow toward. I expedite things by having informal reminders of my dream all around me. For example,
when I wanted to go to New York to write this book and meet
with people in the publishing world, there were logistical and
financial realities to contend with. To help make this dream
happen, my husband bought me a coffee-table book about the
history of Times Square that I saw whenever I sat in the living
room. I found a computer mouse pad that bore a map of the
New York City subway system. I kept a snapshot of the corner
of Seventeenth Street and Eighth Avenue on my nightstand. And
when I got a free minute, I imagined myself there: hailing a taxi,
eating a bagel, smelling the flowers I'd just bought from a
streetside vendor. I was thoroughly *there* in my consciousness,
and that laid the groundwork for getting there in fact. I worked
in practical ways to make it possible, but I also set up a field of
attraction that made its not happening *im*possible. Dream fulfillment takes both inner and outer effort. In my case, that com-
bined endeavor got me an enchanted autumn in Manhattan.

As you use your visual aids and mental imaging, take steps
in the outer world to nurture an embryonic dream into its viable
state. These actions can be small; their power is in the intention
that underlies them. *Know* that your dream is on its way to fulfillment. It may come packaged differently than you'd imagined.
Your timing and life's timing may not be identical. Your dream

may come to you in pieces instead of all at once. Be on the lookout for the pieces.

When your dream does come true, be as focused on its reality as you were on its potential. Fully experience every bit of it, even the parts you didn't bargain for. The baby you want so much *will* keep you up at night; the job you'd give your eyeteeth for *will* make you work longer and harder than you ever have. But this is your dream. Be there for it. All of it.

32

Master Simple Living and High Thinking

*You know that your life is too complicated if you feel
overwhelmed more than twice a month. That allows you
one exemption for PMS and another for living in
a complicated world.*

When your thoughts are lofty and your life is manageable,
you're at the blissful balance point at which human life
works best. Here you're at liberty to be as beautiful, as creative,
and as fulfilled as you were meant to be when you ventured
forth as an eager soul ready to begin your life's adventure.
Many people never get close to this sublime balance of high
thinking and simple living because the mass culture depends on
herd mentality and nonstop acquisition. We're bombarded with
the lie that possessions will make us happy. If we believe this,
we inevitably find ourselves sad, either because we're yearning
endlessly for things we don't have or because we get them and
discover that they can't deliver on their promise.

Simplifying our lives can help, as long as the simplification itself doesn't become another impossible standard to meet. A simple life is not seeing how little we can get by with—that's poverty—but how efficiently we can put first things first. That's where the high thinking comes in. When you're clear about your purpose and your priorities, you can painlessly discard whatever does not support these, whether it's clutter in your cabinets or commitments on your calendar.

You know that your life is too complicated if you feel overwhelmed more than twice a month. That allows you one exemption for PMS and another for living in a complicated world. Beyond that, life should flow smoothly. There will be problems in a simple life, too, because this is earth, not heaven, but the problems won't arise from having too much stuff to take care of or too many promises to keep. To this end:

Establish each day on the firm footing of your ultimate purpose. You are an expression of the eternal, here to do something no one else who has ever lived can do. If you write that at the top of the page in your day planner, you're less likely to get caught up in time-consuming minutiae that cause stress and consume energy.

Do what needs to be done first. It is tempting to do what we want to do before doing what we ought to do. Not so smart—especially now that life is moving at such a rapid pace. Some physicists have hypothesized that the universe itself has sped up. I don't know about that, but days do seem shorter than they used to and there truly isn't time for a lot of excess. Figure out what is important, and proceed accordingly. Top priority for anyone with a serious concern about spiritual matters is to know God or know herself, whichever of those works philosophically. Beyond that, put family, work, friends, education, recreation, causes you support, and upkeep of body, home, and possessions into the mix in an order that makes sense—both for your life in general and today in particular.

Simplify your self-care. Sometimes in fashion magazines you'll read that the beauty routine of some gorgeous model is washing her face with soap from the supermarket, moisturizing with almond oil, and doing no formal exercise other than riding a bike for transportation. It seems unfair or even untrue. Today I believe it. She has found what works for her with the superfluous stripped away. We can do that, too. If some product or practice works for you, stick with it as long as it does. Don't feel the need to gild the lily, regardless of what the woman behind the counter tries to tell you.

Sometimes, practice living with less. It's good to remind ourselves how sweet life can be when we're temporarily freed from the complexity of our comforts. Whether it's camping an hour away for the weekend or trekking in Nepal for a month, these times apart from the trappings of our normal lives show us who we are without embellishment.

The rest of the time, have everything you need to make life function smoothly. If you wear lipstick, it makes sense to have two of the same color so there is one in the bathroom and another in your purse. Well-placed spare keys can be a godsend. Memorabilia of people you love and times you were happiest can make any place you find yourself your own. These necessary accoutrements of a quality life are not the same as saving string or keeping eleven years of back issues of *National Geographic*. You can tell the difference because the things that make life work either get frequent use or make you feel good when you remember you have them. String doesn't do that.

Practice polite refusal to potential intruders on your space and time. Newsletter? No, thank you. Electronic newsletter? No, thank you. Flyer, circular, menu? No, thank you. If you really want to know what they're serving at the Genghis Khan Mongolian Barbecue, take the menu, but practice polite refusal of whatever you do not want clogging up either your tote bag or your day.

You can politely refuse to let a phone call go on at length: "It's been so nice talking with you. I have to hang up now." You can read an e-mail and, unless a response is called for, let it go at that. (I learned this from my husband; he said other people are busy, too, and don't want to spend time reading, "Thanks for your e-mail. Have a nice day," any more than I want to spend time writing it.) And you can politely refuse to be called into service for someone else's passion. Focus on your own passions, and you'll stay busy enough.

PART VI

Quality of Character

3 3

Regard Others as Significant

Perhaps the most pervasive of the many myths of physical attractiveness is that women—or men—are good-looking because they look good. That's not altogether true. They're good-looking because somebody thinks they look good.

Not long ago, I was having lunch with my friend Lane. We were in a Chinese restaurant called the Noodle House that made no mention on the menu of any noodles. Lane and I have known each other for more than ten years. During that time, our two lives have endured a divorce and a breakup, illness and accidents, moves and upheavals. We've been through full plates and empty nests, the death of both our fathers, and the passing of three beloved cats and Daffodil, a revered Labrador. We've supported each other through it all, and when we're together the sad times fade and we laugh a great deal. Across the table Lane searched in vain for a dish with a noodle in it, her glasses perched on her nose, making her look almost as wise as she is. I

looked at her and thought, "This is one beautiful woman." So I told her. "You're crazy," she said, "but thanks anyway."

Lane did not look beautiful to me just because she is my friend and I love her. But because she is my friend and I love her, my brain gets the message "beautiful" every time my eyes deliver the image "Lane." Other people in my life look this comely to me, too, because I admire them, respect them, appreciate them, or have shared so much with them that they just started looking really nice after a while. Perhaps the most pervasive of the many myths of physical attractiveness is that women—or men—are good-looking because they look good. That's not altogether true. They're good-looking because somebody *thinks* they look good.

In the media world, this perception is generated through marketing. "So-and-so is the most beautiful woman in the world," and somebody else is "the sexiest man alive." If we hear this enough, we start to believe it. Then some person who may not have merited a second glance last year becomes the quintessence of beauty or virility. In our personal lives, we at first respond to other people's attractiveness or lack of it based on who in our past they might resemble or how closely they fit whatever standard of beauty we think is our own. After we know them for a while, though, we see more of the person, the one inside. That person, far more than any particulars of face or physique, informs our perception.

People observe us the same way. If you want to look as lovely as your soul knows you are, you have to show some of that soul to others. We often hold back because it's frightening—we

don't want to be known that well—or intimidating: "If she knew the real me, she wouldn't like me." But the real you is the only thing to like. Anything less isn't worth the effort to get to know.

We show our soul to other people by understanding where we fit in this sea of others. The term *significant other* is interesting. Beyond the fact that no one has come up with an acceptable one-word term in English that is more dignified than *boyfriend* or *girlfriend* and less blatant than *lover*, the implication is that only a romantic relationship can make someone a *significant* other. This is absurd. Certainly some people are closer to us than other people are, but everyone is significant, the same way we want to be significant to the many "others" in our lives.

A spiritual teacher once told me that a reasonable goal in life is to see every child the way I would regard my own son or daughter. I wasn't even a parent yet when I heard that, but I somehow realized anyway this feat would be just about impossible to achieve. When I think I'm flying high, I remember the objective I'm supposed to be shooting for and get back to reality in short order. Even so, between here and where I want to be, I can at least regard other people as significant. I can do the best I'm able to today to be a positive "other" to those closest to me and to the rest of the world. "Other" is our biggest role anyway: we're only "me" to one person on earth; we're "other" to an entire planet.

To allow the people around us their due significance, we can do the following:

Follow through on positive inclinations. If it crosses your mind that you ought to call a particular friend or you feel moved to give money to a particular street person even if you usually give only to established charities, go ahead. Your soul can't put up billboards; it has to reach you through nudges that, as busy as people get, can be easy to miss.

Support other people the way they want to be supported. This is easier to do with other women than with men, I think, and it's sometimes hardest with husbands and boyfriends. What can these very different human beings possibly want? Ask them. Watch them. Pay attention. See how they support you. It's probably how they want to be supported. Some people are pragmatic; they're looking for answers, solutions, and accomplished tasks. Others are philosophical; they like ideas, musings, and metaphors. Just about everybody hopes to be heard when they want to talk and left alone when they don't.

See the beauty in people. All my friends are beautiful. Of course they're various shapes, sizes, ages, and types, but each one of them is absolutely gorgeous to me. You know how in high school it's a big status thing to hang out with the pretty girls? It was long after high school that I finally made it to the "in crowd" by realizing that seeking my own inner light would draw to me people who are seeking theirs. They are unique and extraordinary individuals. I feel so blessed to be around any of them and jubilant when several are present at once. Heaven has to be where you can have all your friends in one place.

Be generous with heartfelt compliments. A kind word can make a person's day—and can make her feel significant. You can tell the difference between a compliment that comes from your heart and one that you're stretching to come up with or that you feel you owe. The heartfelt ones feel as if they're welling up from inside you. The sensation is almost physical. You have a real desire to share something positive with another person, whether this "other" is your own mother or the guy who just delivered the pizza.

Keep in touch. The people who are most significant to us need to know that they are. This is why it's important to keep in touch. It's harder than it once was because so many of us live in a variety of places over the course of our lives and thereby make more friends than our ancestors could have dreamed of having. Some people do come into our lives for only a certain period; we grow apart and that's the way of things. But notes and calls and cards can be a lifeline to those it would be a shame to lose. I carry postcards in my day planner so when I have to wait for an appointment I can write to someone I don't regularly see. E-mail helps people stay connected, too, as long as you avoid inundation by keeping messages short and deleting the junk mail and forwards.

Be a good friend. Be the kind of friend you want for yourself. Listen. Show up. Keep confidences. Mend fences before you trip over one. And regardless of what friends are thinking or doing, stay true to yourself. That gives everyone who knows you permission to be true to themselves, too.

34

Become Magnanimous

Magnanimity is rising above your ego-self. It's living beyond pettiness and displaying courage and generosity.

Frankie was struggling with a situation at work. "I'm sick of always taking the high road," she told me. She took it anyway, one more time. It didn't surprise me; Frankie has character. She knows where to go for inner guidance when she needs it, and she has a radiance you could pick out in a stadium. Frankie is the only woman I know who, when going through a divorce she didn't ask for, actually looked better than usual. We went to lunch the day her divorce became final, and a well-dressed gentleman walked right up to our table and asked her out. She declined, explaining that she was probably fifteen years older than he. It turned out to be twenty.

Frankie's beauty secret is, I think, magnanimity. In addition to being a pretty good tongue twister, magnanimity is rising above your ego-self. It's living beyond pettiness and displaying courage and generosity. When your magnanimity comes from a position of soul strength, you don't give up because you're weak or give in because you're afraid. When something is important, you hold your ground. When it isn't, you let it go with grace and dignity.

You're being magnanimous every time you make the first move to end a quarrel and every time you let a bygone stay gone. You show this quality whenever you do something noble and keep quiet about it. And when you do a service for another person, responding to their thanks with "My pleasure" and realizing that it really was a pleasure, you know you've got it.

Something as simple as giving in on a meaningless point and letting someone else be right can be magnanimity par excellence. For people whose inner resources are very low, being right seems to temporarily fill the empty spaces, the way a starving person might drink water to temporarily fill the stomach. As you become more magnanimous, you grow to understand that some people, although housing the same divine light as your own, have no idea that it's in there.

Like children with whom we're patient because they have little life experience, many adults seem to have little soul experience. Some people would say that's because they haven't lived many lives on earth; others would say they simply haven't paid much attention to inner matters during the life they have now.

Either way, these people give us a wonderful opportunity to become more magnanimous.

Another aspect of magnanimity is giving freely. Giving opens your account with the abundance of the universe. Living in abundance makes you relaxed and at ease. Wealthy women look good not just because they can afford designer clothes, frequent facials, and cosmetic surgery; they're free to look lovely because they live in the safety of abundance. We can all share in that safety without winning any sweepstakes or getting lucky in the stock market. In day-to-day life, it can be as simple as rounding the tip *up* to the nearest dollar or, when you're out with friends, refusing to wrestle with the restaurant bill until it's divided with mathematical precision. Loosen up. Put in the extra buck. Become magnanimous. Give little gifts to people you care about. Give to charities you believe in and spiritual centers that nourish your soul.

Have the nerve to tithe, giving 10 percent of your income to a church, to someone in need, or some institution doing valuable work. Tithing allows you do good and feel rich at the same time. When you think it's causing you to give a little more than is practical, you have to depend on a higher source to make up the difference. When you can trust this much, you know you're living in the light.

Besides, nobody can outgive God. While most people are concerned with stretching their paycheck to cover their needs and wants, tithers look for wonderful places to share. Those who tithe consistently assert that they invariably end up with more money after tithing than they had before. The process of regular giving seems to open invisible floodgates, clearing blocked channels so the spiritual law of receiving in proportion to giving works clearly to their benefit. They stop worrying about money, and soon there is nothing to worry about.

As you become more magnanimous, in even the smallest ways, you'll be given more opportunities to show the qualities you've developed. One day you'll realize you've become the person you set out to be. Nothing feels better than that.

35

Understand: "Beauty Is Truth and Truth Beauty"

Truthfulness is pretty simple; it's not fictionalizing reality.

I was five years old when I told my first lie. I came home from kindergarten, and Dede, the woman who looked after me, asked what my class had done that day. The same old "coloring, songs, and snack" sounded so mundane. Then I remembered that the fourth and fifth graders got to go once a week to a stable for riding lessons, and I blurted out, "We rode horses." I instantly felt that I'd just been expelled from Eden with Adam and Eve. With those three words, I left innocence behind me and I knew it. Sitting at the kitchen table with two sandwich cookies and a glass of milk, I had the strange sense that my childhood had just ended.

Subsequent lies didn't have nearly the effect of that first one, and I grew into depending on exaggerations, half-truths, fabricated excuses, and self-deluding rationalizations to make me feel more important, get me out of what I didn't want to do, or save face. In retrospect, they never saved anything, but they did become so natural that when a spiritual director told me, "Don't lie, period, ever, for any reason," I was amazed by his fervor on the subject. "God is truth," he told me, "and the only way you can get to God is through the truth. If you don't want to do that, stop wasting my time."

His truthfulness formula was (1) to clear up any damage done by past untruths as best I could; (2) to commit to speaking the truth and admit it immediately when I missed the mark, which he assured me I would; and (3) to accept the truth—about myself, my past, my present, and my circumstances. I tried, failing every bit as often as he'd said I would. But after a while, my life felt cleaner, lighter. It wasn't quite like returning to the golden time before the horseback-riding tale, but I knew that if I stayed firm in my resolve, it would bring me as close to that as I could get.

Truthfulness is pretty simple; it's not fictionalizing reality. It's also being open to a higher degree of truth than what may be visible in the moment—like working with the affirmations in chapter 3. Truthfulness should never be used as an excuse to hurt another person; it also does not require telling anyone anything that is none of their business. What honesty does ask is that we speak truthfully when we choose to speak; that we temper our words with all the kindness we can muster; and that we look at reality straight on, accept what we've got, and build from there.

36

Be Trustworthy and Tolerant

Inner glow rises from inner conviction.

If honesty is the truthfulness we speak, trustworthiness is the
truthfulness we live. What a sweet state to be in, to be worthy of the trust of those around us! It's pragmatic and to the
point. We develop more of it every time we show up where we
say we'll be, do what we say we'll do, pay what we owe, and
follow through on a promise to another person or to ourselves.

The first step toward increased trustworthiness is to under-
take less so you can follow through on more. Promise *less* than
you know you can do so you'll be able to meet or even exceed
expectations. Schedule appointments with time to spare; it will
save you the anxiety of being rushed and may give you extra

minutes to collect yourself, read, write, or make a call. Aim to be sincere, even in something as nonchalant as "Let's have lunch."

Next, see yourself as a trustworthy human being. We tend to reach toward the standards we set for ourselves; setting them is the key. Think of yourself as a person of integrity, and watch your actions meet your expectations. Finally, value trustworthiness for its own sake. Introduce into your own vocabulary those marvelous, old-fashioned words your grandmother might have used: *upright, aboveboard, honorable, foursquare, solid, high-minded.* Think of what it means to have "good character," to be the "salt of the earth," "honest as the day is long," and "as good as your word." When my daughter was learning to read, I ordered her a reprinted version of the 1800s *McGuffey Reader* because these principles were imbedded in the stories and vocabulary. We can do this for ourselves by reading biographies of people we admire and fiction in which character triumphs and by seeing films in which the good guys—or the good women—win.

As you increasingly build more character, beware of one caveat: self-righteousness would love to join the party; tolerance is what will keep it out. Curiously, ethical precepts go in and out of favor like vacation spots and cocktails. Tolerance is not highly regarded in many circles now because it's seen as weak, as not standing for anything. On the contrary, true tolerance is standing so firmly for what you believe that you have no problem allowing others to do the same.

In college, I took a class about Islam taught by a Christian clergyman. He explained Muslim teachings with such depth of understanding, such admiration, and such passion that a student asked him why he didn't just convert. He answered, "I appreciate Muhammad, but I resonate with Jesus." So *that* was tolerance: appreciating someone else's truth while resonating with your own. I took two more courses from that professor, and he taught both Judaism and Buddhism with the same fair-mindedness and respect he had shown in the class on Islam.

None of us knows how we would see the world if we had been born in a different family, not to mention a different culture. None of us is wise enough to be intolerant. This does not mean refusing to stand up for what we believe; that's an obligation. We have to do it, however, in a way that does not diminish someone else.

This is all so serious when we're supposed to be talking about inner glow. But inner glow rises from inner conviction. That's not always easily come by, but when you have it, it's yours to keep.

37

Forgive Someone Something

Forgive someone something. . . . You'll feel closer to what's divine because you'll be doing something that is divine.

Grudges make a person grumpy, and that's not becoming. Unforgiving people scowl, and the lines that form as they grow older aren't the wonderful crinkles that indicate years of laughter, tears, and fine memories. They're more like furrows drawn by some injustice, whether real or imagined. Phrases like "carry a grudge" and "hold a resentment" are literally true: people hold them in their faces and carry them in their posture. Letting these go results in an immediate freeing up of energy. Eventually, you'll want to forgive almost everyone for almost everything. Today, just forgive someone something.

In Alcoholics Anonymous, members talk about praying that the person they resent be given everything they themselves want.

It's a simple process: "God, please let Joan land that job in Hawaii, get along well with her kids, and be able to buy a BMW—forest green." Joan may not even like forest green, but praying for *her* to have what *you* want opens your heart in a miraculous way. You'll feel closer to what's divine because you'll be doing something that is divine. You'll be channeling grace into the life of someone else, someone your human ego would prefer to see driving a broken-down compact with see-through rust spots.

Forgiveness is a little bit for the other person. No one functions at her best when negative thoughts are beamed at her non-stop. Recognizing this probably led to the old superstition about putting curses on people. Still, the effect of your resentment on the other person is too subtle to even qualify as satisfying revenge. You may as well let go of it altogether. Besides, you will be the one to get the most from the process since you've been carrying the baggage.

Some time ago, I was told that I needed to do some major forgiveness work. I was supposed to make a list of everybody I resented and make things right. I could get by with writing a sincere letter to anyone on the list who was no longer living, and I could telephone the people who lived far away. Anyone who was alive and within five hundred miles, however, I was supposed to go to in person. Oh—and I couldn't say, "I resent you because you stole my lunch box in kindergarten." I was supposed to make amends for what I had done to offend them. "You'll be sweeping your side of the street," my mentor told me.

My side of the street seemed like the westbound interstate. Still, I made my way from person to person. There were some touching encounters, some uncomfortable exchanges, and an agonizing two hours with my father, now deceased. He vented every angry thought he'd ever had and ended with, "Good. I'm glad we had this talk."

When it was all over, I started the eight-hour drive back home. I felt exhausted but free. And clean, too, the way you feel when you've just had your teeth cleaned and haven't yet had any coffee or grape juice. At the last tollbooth, the quarters went flying, missing their target. The attendant started to say, "You're still responsible for . . ." Then he caught my eye, stopped for a moment, and said, "No, you don't have to pay. I know you intended to. Besides, you're just so beautiful."

I know he meant that in the pure, detached way that we mean things when they're simply facts or when we think they are. I also know that I was not then and have never been "beautiful" in the objective way that some women are. The man at the tollbooth that summer evening saw something else. He saw my inner light because, for a time, it was extraordinarily bright. He interpreted that as beautiful because that's how it looked to him.

Since the inner light is our essence, it inevitably shows up when whatever has been hiding it is eliminated, the way Michelangelo carved from the stone everything that wasn't David. Resentments and unforgiving thoughts cover the light more completely than anything else. Still, forgiving is not the easiest thing you'll ever do. There is no guarantee that there will be any parity to it, that the people you forgive will open their hearts as widely as you have, if they open them at all. This is one dance you have to be willing to do on your own. The people you forgive, whether in their presence or in your own mind, may not change one iota. Either way, you can stop lugging the burden.

Today, forgive someone something. If you like how it feels, forgive another person tomorrow. Don't start by trying to forgive somebody for the most awful pain you've ever suffered. It takes tremendous spiritual depth to forgive that thoroughly. I read that Mahatma Gandhi never pressed charges the many times he was brutally assaulted. "They thought what they were doing was right," he said. I am certainly not at that point in my spiritual evolution. If you aren't either, don't worry about it. We don't expect fourth graders to do calculus. On the other hand, we don't let them off without knowing long division. Forgive what you can today. Allow your capacity for doing it to increase.

And while you're at it, please forgive yourself. Louise Hay has written, "If we feel we are not 'good enough,' it is only because we have not yet forgiven ourselves." Of course you've done rotten things. We all have. A realistic aim is to avoid doing the same rotten things over again. If you owe someone money, pay it. If you owe an apology, make it. If there is anything you can do in your present life that would right a past wrong without hurting someone else, do all you can. Then sincerely ask the God of your understanding to forgive you. He, She, or It will gladly do that; in fact, He, She, or It already has. If God can forgive you, it's probably all right for you to forgive you, too.

38

Go Graciously Through Your Day

Graciousness is acting on the belief that we have been given adequate time and ability to care for one another.

Graciousness is treating other people as if they're worth as much as you are. It will earn you the admiration of friends and the gratitude of strangers. I'm sure this is the trait that started the notion of "pretty is as pretty does" because, although graciousness may not alter your features or your figure, it does change the way people see you.

I know of a children's librarian who loves kids more than anything and books almost as much. During one of her weekend story hours, a five-year-old boy was waving his arm wildly, demanding to be heard. She stopped her reading to ask, "Is it important?" He assured her that it was. "Go ahead then," she said. He looked at her intently for a few seconds and then spoke: "You are very beautiful." None of the other children laughed or disputed his statement because they agreed with it. If you were to get a copy of that librarian's medical chart, you would see her described with the words *morbidly obese*. For those to whom she gives a world of wonder every Saturday morning, that makes no difference. She is beautiful. End of discussion.

The children's opinion of their beloved "story lady" comes from the appreciation, compassion, and courtesy she shows them. Grown-ups respond to appreciation, compassion, and courtesy, too. We all think well of a person who notices our efforts, validates our opinions, or takes our concerns seriously. We love it when somebody takes time for us, even if it's just to wait for our answer to the ubiquitous query, "How are you?" This is what graciousness is: acting on the belief that we have been given adequate time and ability to care for one another.

Putting more graciousness into your dealings with other people can be gratifying for you and everyone around you. You already know how to do it. Your mother probably taught you before you went to kindergarten, and you probably taught your dolls. If you haven't been as gracious lately as you'd like to be, it's probably because life is so hectic. When chaos comes in, cordiality is the first thing to go. Get it back with time to spare by looking for ways to add kindness and even a little gentility to what you're already doing. Try some of these suggestions and add your own:

Be polite. When you don't know someone, be polite. When you don't like someone, be polite. When you feel uncomfortable, out of place, or at a loss for words, just be polite. It doesn't take learning the fine points of etiquette. Politeness is simply respecting, and at times deferring to, another person. Many of us have been so thoroughly trained in assertiveness that we think letting someone get on the bus ahead of us is denying our worth. Not so. It's having enough worth that little things get to be little.

Call people by name. Everybody loves to be personally addressed. You can do this with friends, colleagues, service people wearing name tags, and others you talk to only by phone. Sometimes when you've been put through the wringer by a voice-mail system that made you press 103 buttons to get to a human, it's hard to remember that this person you finally talk to really *is* human. Using his name or her name will help. It will also endear you to someone whose job is to assist faceless and often aggravated customers all day long.

Give anyone who wants your help a set amount of time. This is how you can be gracious and still have a life. Otherwise, you go from being gracious to being used. I usually turn off the phone when I'm writing, but sometimes I forget and answer it as a reflex action. When the person on the other end has a problem, I say something like, "I can only give you ten minutes now, but for those ten minutes, I'm all yours." And I am. When the ten minutes is up, they're up. I tell them, "This is all the time I have. If you need to talk again, I'll be free this evening between seven-thirty and eight."

Show up for other people's high times and low ones. We're all busy. These days, people rarely "stop by to chat," and we'd probably be annoyed if they did. Nevertheless, a gracious person is there for friends and acquaintances in times of both sadness and success. It is important to be present for showers and funerals, to toast a promotion or lament a termination, to listen to a friend who's in love and to another who's lost a love. If you can't be on hand in person, be there by proxy with flowers, a letter, or an invitation to get together in the near future. Note on your calendar important days in other people's lives, and keep a supply of cards in your drawer so you always have an appropriate one to send.

Do for a peripheral person what you would do for a close one. I excused myself from a business breakfast early because I had an appointment for an MRI; some of the things that had to be ruled out were quite scary. "You're going alone?" Elizabeth asked. She was a woman I'd met maybe three times; we were definitely peripheral people in each other's lives at that point. Nevertheless, when she heard that I was going for the procedure by myself, she called her office, rearranged her schedule, and went with me. The results were not dire—I had a herniated disc from an old car accident—and I made a dear friend who taught me that you don't have to have history with somebody to come through for them.

See things from the other person's point of view. If your baby starts to cry or you're dying for a cigarette or a call comes in on your cell phone, go someplace where other people won't be bothered. Be a courteous driver: park so the car behind you can be gotten out easily; if there is just not enough room, park on the next block. Don't pass along jokes that are offensive to *anybody;* you don't know who's listening, and that kind of joke only makes the teller look bad. Appreciate other people's hobbies and interests, hopes and dreams, whether they're similar to yours or very different. And when someone is in distress, even over something that seems minor to you, listen and empathize as best you can.

Do something surprising. One of my fondest childhood memories is coming home from school one autumn afternoon and finding that my mother had put together a "half-birthday party" to mark my turning six and a half. Even with fewer presents and less hoopla than a real birthday, it meant more because I hadn't expected it. It works for adults, too. Surprise somebody with a little gift, a special lunch, tickets to a play, whatever you know she'd like and probably wouldn't do for herself.

Take an interest in people. Everyone has a story. Most people have dozens. When you take an interest in their lives, you let them take center stage for a while, a place many people rarely get to be. And learning about another person's world makes yours bigger.

Let other people be gracious to you. Sometimes it's hard to just say thank you and let yourself receive a gift, a compliment, or some service from another person. Do it, even if doing so feels a bit uncomfortable. After a while, these things will make you feel terrific because you'll see they're not about you in an ego sense at all. They are rather a way for love to take on form. That's what inner beauty is all about: love with dimensions. Extend it and accept it.

PART VII

Nourishing Yourself

39

Invite Your Soul to Dinner

Dine with gratitude. And Mozart.

You've heard that eating "keeps body and soul together." This is a sacred mission. We are nourished not only by the food but also by the ambience surrounding it. When we're calm and in good spirits, we assimilate nutrients more efficiently. When we're tense, angry, or tired, the body is less able to direct needed energy to the digestive process.

Saying grace or having a little space of silence before eating is one way to put us in the right frame of mind. It provides an interlude to relax for a minute, to breathe more deeply, to remember where we fit in the grand scheme of things. A blessing on the meal may even enhance the food itself. In one study, highly skilled yogis were able to select from an array of dishes those that had received the benefit of prayer. Saying a prayer before fixing food is also a worthy practice since, according to yogic teachings, a centered, content cook imparts those qualities to whatever is being prepared.

Unfortunately, food preparation, prayerful or not, is becoming a lost art except among professional chefs. Some people never learned how to cook, and many who did are either tired of doing it or too busy for anything that a microwave can't turn into a meal. If you don't know slice from dice, take a course in basic cooking; or get out of a culinary rut with a class in gourmet or ethnic or natural foods cuisine.

If you're too busy to give time and care to food preparation, frequent restaurants where *someone* is giving it time and care, or hire a conscientious caterer a few nights a week. If you can't afford to, ask yourself: Why am I devoting so much time to a job that doesn't offer sufficient compensation for me to eat well? It is vitally important that you have the time to prepare healthy food, or another willing person in your household has the time to do it, or you're trading your time for enough money to pay someone else for this service.

And when wonderful food is in front of you, savor it. I was delighted recently when a restaurant server didn't ask about clearing the dishes with the customary, "Are you still working on that?" He asked instead, "Are you still enjoying this?" It was an entirely different question. It invited me to slow down, and that is the first step toward eating in a way that acknowledges the soul as well as the body. We are too valuable to "grab a bite." If there isn't time for a full meal, have an abridged version, but sit down for it. Focus on it. Relax with it. The belief in India is that eating hurriedly causes toxins to build up in the system and that outward signs of aging are, in large part, a result of this self-pollution.

So take a little time, even if it's only fifteen minutes for breakfast, thirty for lunch, and forty-five for dinner. That's an hour and a half a day—50 percent of the time most people spend watching television—devoted to maintaining the only body you get in this life. Dine with gratitude. And Mozart. Anticipate a level of gustatory pleasure you may have forgotten. Expect weight worries to lessen as you give your body what it needs, and give yourself the sensory satisfaction some people frantically search for in oversized cookies and half-gallons of ice cream.

Pass this attitude on to your children as well. They deserve better than phony food packed in plastic and aluminum and cardboard, even if that's what savvy marketers have convinced them they want. We do children an enormous disservice when we assume that they cannot appreciate anything beyond drive-through fare and nutritionally marginal, kid-targeted convenience foods. Our children are capable of consuming something that grew in a garden or on a tree and never saw a deep fryer. They are capable of making it through dinner at a sit-down restaurant with tablecloths and no climbing equipment. Children deserve quality nourishment because they're light bearers, just like we are. If anything, they're *closer* to that light since they came from it such a short time ago.

We care for both ourselves and our loved ones by choosing real food and presenting it in a civilized way. This is not to say that there is never a time for carnival food or ballpark food or birthday party food. Of course there is. But for the day to day, strive for the highest quality you can come by. Consider:

Serious bread. This is bread that a human being baked and you cut yourself or break apart and share. Whole-grain bread is nutritionally superior, but even white bread that was kneaded by human hands gives you something its factory-produced cousin can't. Serve it with virgin olive oil like the Italians.

Fresh greens. Buy field greens washed and ready to eat. And splurge sometimes on a little package of edible flowers. Nobody can turn down a salad that has violets and nasturtiums in it.

Cloth napkins. You can often find them at yard sales. Give everybody in the family his or her own in a distinctive napkin ring; that way they last a week.

Flowers on the table. Carnations and daisies are cheerful and cheap, and if you change the water every few days, they can last two weeks.

Stemmed goblets. I get mine for three dollars apiece, so breaking one is no big deal. They needn't be saved for wine. Bring them out for mineral water, sparkling cider, and morning smoothies. Whatever you're drinking, the stem makes it special.

The art of conversation. You won't digest properly, much less enjoy the meal, if there is argument or discord at the table. Save *discussions* (you know those: heavy talks about work, finances, major decisions, and the like) for another time. Dinner is for *conversation* about the events of the day, movies, plays, fun things coming up.

Dressing for dinner. I know, as busy as everybody is, this is almost laughable. But I'm not suggesting formal attire, just something fresh and different from what you wore all day. I was once told, "Dress for any occasion to show the respect you have for it." Sustaining a body and connecting with the people who make your life worthwhile are certainly worthy of respect—and a clean shirt.

40

Dine like a Yogi

Simple, natural foods produce the glow of good health as evidenced by radiant skin, a strong, flexible body, and a well-functioning immune system.

The state of our bodies is genetically destined to some degree. The rest we construct ourselves, largely from the food we eat. Experts and mock experts debate ceaselessly about how we ought to feed ourselves, and diets go in and out of style more rapidly than hemlines or hairdos. Yoga philosophy, however, which has always had a lot to say about living physical life in accordance with spiritual laws, hasn't changed its basic dietary recommendation for over two thousand years. It is: *Choose pure foods, and enjoy them in moderate amounts.*

The yogis classify foods, and everything else for that matter, in groups called *gunas,* the basic characteristics of creation. The three *gunas* are *tamasic,* the quality of gravity; *rajasic,* the quality of motion; and *sattvic,* the quality of light.

Tamasic foods are those considered lifeless. They include anything stale or tasteless; leftovers of more than twenty-four hours and anything that's been in the freezer for a long time; also aged cheese, alcoholic beverages, deep-fried fare, and all highly processed foods with chemical additives. The teaching is that too many of these promote lethargy and fatigue and lessen our sensitivity to beauty and virtue. *Rajasic* foods—meat, eggs, refined sugar and soft drinks, stimulants like coffee, and dishes with fiery spices and lots of salt—set our body rhythms at full speed ahead. When taken in excess, these can add to our stress levels and make us driven and high-strung.

Balancing these two extremes are the simple, natural *sattvic* foods, including fresh fruits, raw or lightly cooked vegetables, whole grains and brown breads, beans, nuts, honey, and milk from healthy cows. It is believed that eating predominantly sattvic foods is healing and calming, sharpens the mind, supports spiritual growth, and keeps the body's channels clean. This produces the glow of good health as evidenced by radiant skin, a strong, flexible body, and a well-functioning immune system. The ancient Indians had a name for this glow, *ojas,* which they defined as the physiologic expression of bliss: a nonstop, underlying happiness that persists even through trying times. Foods said to be especially *ojas* producing include:

Barley: You can buy whole barley at a natural food store and prepare it as a hot cereal or use it in soup to replace rice or noodles;

Basmati rice: An aromatic, nutty-flavored rice available in both brown and white varieties at most supermarkets;

Mung beans: The bean sprouts used in Chinese cooking are usually mung bean sprouts; you can also buy quick-cooking *mung dhal,* split mung beans, at Indian markets and some grocery stores;

Sesame seeds: Toss a tablespoon into a smoothie or sprinkle some on a salad; discover tahini (sesame butter) and halvah (sesame candy) at health food stores and in the foreign foods aisle of the supermarket;

Blanched almonds: Buy them already blanched (they're sold inexpensively in the bulk barrels at many natural foods stores), or buy plain raw almonds, cover them with boiling water, let them sit a couple of minutes, and pop off the skins yourself;

Fresh fruits, particularly dates, figs, and oranges: Buy organically grown fruit whenever you can; grapes, peaches, apples, pears, and berries tend to be heavily sprayed and should be organic if at all possible. When you're buying dried fruit like figs, look for the kind that have no sulphur added. Because dried fruit is very sweet, you may want to soak it in pure water for a few hours so it more nearly resembles its fresh state when you eat it.

Good food choices are half of the yogic dietary equation. The other is moderation. A commentary on the Bhagavad Gita reads, "Even nectar becomes poison when eaten too much." Modern science concurs, noting that a common theme among people who live healthfully into their nineties and beyond is a lifetime of moderate eating. Moderation is actually the flip side of dieting, that is, imposed deprivation. It is instead choosing foods that are so delicious, so delightful to look at and to smell, and so satisfying to the appetite and to the body's trillions of nutrition-seeking cells that the need to overeat can be arrested at its source.

An additional way to guard against eating to excess is to give your body digestion time between meals. Nonstop eating causes more than weight gain: it causes energy loss. Digesting food is an energy-intensive process. Piling more food on top of what hasn't been digested yet hinders the process, causing fatigue. Some people have medical conditions that require them to eat frequently, but the rest of us would do well to take the yogic path and stick with three meals a day. "Nothing in between?" I asked my first yoga teacher, somewhat shocked, when she suggested this. "Living in between," she told me.

41

Consider a Gentler Diet

Choose food that is as beautiful as you wish to be yourself.

Animals are amazing. They seem to live unpretentiously in the moment and love unconditionally. They can calm us down, and statistics reveal that people who live with them have greater longevity and superior health profiles than those in humans-only households. People who love their dogs and cats know that these companions have thoughts, emotions, and memories. It follows that other mammals are similarly equipped. When a person feels this at a soul level, she takes seriously the words of the ancient Indian sage Mahavira: "To every creature, its own life is very dear." When this happens, she may no longer be comfortable eating meat.

For some women, this is a step on their path to more fully expressing their inner beauty. It is by no means required; as in everything else, following your inner guidance is of utmost importance. If, however, you have vegetarian sensibilities, following through on them can help you become more beautiful, body and soul. You may have vegetarian sensibilities if you love animals or simply hate the thought of their suffering. If movies like *Bambi* or *Babe* or *Chicken Run* either make you cry or make you think, you probably have them, too. And if you've ever thought that you would like to stop eating meat "someday," those are vegetarian sensibilities cropping up.

If you have them, allow yourself to adopt a gentler diet. You can do this all at once or gradually, selecting meatless meals more and more often until you find that you've become a vegetarian with seamless ease. Eat a varied diet of natural foods. The basics of a healthy vegetarian food plan are whole grains, vegetables, fruits, beans, and nuts. Some vegetarians eat eggs and use dairy products; others don't. You can be healthy either way. Read up on the subject, and, most of all, pay attention to your body. It knows what it needs and will tell you if you listen. It's a good idea for anyone to take a daily vitamin and mineral supplement, and pure vegetarians do need to supplement vitamin B_{12}. Otherwise, dine from the bounty of nature, and you'll be fine.

Statistically, vegetarians are leaner and healthier than the rest of the population. They live longer and succumb less readily to heart disease and many types of cancer. New vegetarians often release extra weight without a moment's thought to the matter. Other common occurrences are clearer skin, better sleep, heightened energy, and fewer colds. These benefits are believed to come from vegetarians' consuming less fat and cholesterol than meat eaters and more vitamins, minerals, and phytochemicals from fruits and vegetables. I believe that at least part of the reason vegetarians have such vitality is that they're making the world a kinder place and reaping the rewards of that service.

So who should try this? You—if the idea speaks to your heart. Listen to yourself at the deepest level you can. Then nourish yourself in a way that aligns with your soul's design. Choose food that is as beautiful as you wish to be yourself: bright green greenery, brilliant berries, and whole grains that haven't been robbed of their germ and their bran. If you're leaning toward a meatless diet, invest in a vegetarian cookbook that includes a basic nutrition section. Learn the fundamentals. Experiment with new dishes. Or go to restaurants where meat doesn't make the meal. In addition to natural foods cafés, most ethnic restaurants—Asian, Mediterranean, Indian, Ethiopian, and so forth—offer delicious dishes centered around vegetables, grains, beans, and enticing spices from every corner of the planet.

Whatever your dietary choices, make them consciously and reverently. If you eat meat, buy organic meat from a natural food store, co-op, or from a farm you can visit yourself. The meat will be healthier for you and more likely to come from animals who lived until they died instead of existing as production units. Choose vegetables and fruits that lived well, too. I was saddened at an exhibit about hydroponic horticulture when

I saw poor little tomato plants with naked, exposed roots that must have craved, however a plant might, the warmth of soil.

Make your changes graciously, with respect for those around you. No one appreciates dietary evangelism. Instead, invite people over for some satisfying food. Chili sans carne, fresh vegetable stir-fry, mushroom stroganoff, or black bean soup with brown bread and tossed salad are easy to make and complete in themselves; no one will wonder where the meat went.

If someone asks why your skin looks so nice or notices that you've lost a little weight, tell them you're eating more vegetables. For most people who bring it up, that's enough. If someone wants to know more, they'll keeping asking. And when you say grace over your next meal, this prayer from the ancient Vedas would be fitting: "May all beings be relieved of suffering. May the world be filled with peace and joy."

42

Get Past the Weight Thing

Put your focus on living instead of waiting until some scale says that living is allowed.

I f you eat the foods nature provided, and if you move through your life using your arms and legs and muscles as nature intended, you will have the body nature meant for you to have. It will be as nearly perfect as it can be because it will closely approximate what its designer had in mind. It is unlikely that you will have the proportions of a high-fashion model—I've read that only 3 percent of women do—but you will have the ideal proportions for you.

A grassroots movement is burgeoning to emancipate people of size from discrimination and recrimination. This is necessary and important. The other side of the coin, however, is that people who carry so much weight that their joints and hearts can't bear the burden should be as free to reach a healthier state as they are to live without ridicule. One cannot happen without the other. When being overweight is decriminalized in the collective consciousness, we will all feel more comfortable in our skin.

In a personal sense, your body has a place where it would like to settle. (I say "place" rather than "weight" because body weight includes bones and muscle and water and makes women panic for no good reason.) If bodies had their way, many would be thinner than they are now because lots of them have too much fat from a health standpoint. Other bodies would appreciate having more weight and getting more food, and lots would simply like to be left alone the way they are and not periodically prodded into losing five pounds.

The ancient Indian healing system of Ayurveda classifies bodies into three equally desirable types called *doshas*. The *Vata* type is slender and delicate, the *Pitta* type solid and strong, the *Kapha* type curvy and voluptuous. Most of us are a combination of these, with one or two predominating and infinite variables making every body unique. It is possible to work against your body type—a *Vata* can overeat and gain weight, or a *Kapha* can diet to unnatural thinness—but this puts you and your body at odds. Some people are at their healthy best carrying more weight, others less. Accept your anatomy. Then all you have to do is take good care of it.

The wonderful thing about treating yourself well and letting your body be the size and shape it's supposed to be is that this is the size and shape at which you can stop worrying about size and shape. Many women miss out on the joy, healthiness, and self-esteem of being their right size because they have another goal in mind. Whoever invented the concept of "goal weight" ought to go down in infamy. It's not up to us to decide what we're supposed to weigh. How about a "goal height"? Let's see: "This five-foot-five stuff isn't cutting it; I shall strive to be five-eleven." A goal weight is just as silly. Sure, you can reach it— "122 pounds! This calls for strains of 'The Hallelujah Chorus' followed by 'Pomp and Circumstance'"—but you're not going to stay at any weight below which your body feels safe. The drive for self-preservation is too strong.

And if maintaining some arbitrary weight means that you're chronically hungry or depriving yourself of necessary nutrients or just doing without normal social outlets and the enjoyment of food, then that number on the scale you worked so hard to reach is not long for this world. We've been told for so long that thin is good and thinner is better that we have forgotten how to listen to the leading authority on the body: the body itself. We trust it to beat its heart, flow its blood, develop strategies for immune defense, and perform myriad other feats we could not possibly orchestrate. To get past the weight thing, we have to trust that this same brilliant body knows the size it's supposed to be. This will change with circumstances; pregnancy, nursing, monthly cycles, and menopause all shift the shape, especially around the midsection. It's not awful. It's having a life in the kind of body that can give life.

Our job in all this is to refrain from hindering the process. We impede the body in coming to its right size and shape in the following ways:

Eating for a fix. This is unhealthy, emotionally motivated eating. If you do it, it's unlikely that you'll be able to stop on your own. I strongly recommend Overeaters Anonymous. Since problems with eating can have roots deeply embedded in the psyche, a counselor with solid experience in this area can in some cases be invaluable as well.

Believing the standard American diet is normal. The typical American diet, now being franchised to the rest of the world, looks normal only because it's all around us. The typical diet is so artificially colored, flavored, and preserved, so fatty and sweetened and fried and refined, that only a fraction of it is the kind of food that human bodies have come to trust over thousands of years of adaptation. These nonfoods leave the body starving, even when it's stuffed. They can also cause cravings— making you feel hungrier than before you ate.

Giving in to a sedentary lifestyle. The body is a machine designed for vigorous and at times rigorous activity. Offices, automobiles, televisions, and most suburbs are, by definition, fattening. We need to offset their influence with walking, participation in a sport, or exercise we like enough to actually do.

Dieting. The body interprets dieting as, "I'm in the midst of a famine. As soon as the privation lets up, I'd better hold on to every calorie I can get." And it does. This is why diets are such dismal failures. Eating more healthfully every day makes sense. Going on a diet to lose weight doesn't.

"Watching" your weight. In spiritual terms, what could be more inane, in a world with so much need and so many places to put our efforts and our love, than expending mental energy

keeping track of numbers on a scale? Instead of watching your weight, watch the sun rise. Watch your garden grow. Watch your nephew so your sister can get away for the weekend. This puts your focus on living instead of waiting until some scale tells you that living is allowed.

With these five saboteurs out of your life, you get past the weight thing by being kind to yourself and involved with life. Choose healthy foods. Get enjoyable exercise. Have adventures. Make a difference. And dump the goal weight. Every healthy, happy person is uniquely beautiful. You can work on the healthy, happy part. Let your body deal with the weights and measures.

43

Stay Hydrated

At the cellular level, dehydration makes us as droopy as a neglected philodendron.

I learned the importance of hydration from my twenty-year-old cat, Henrietta. At her advanced age, her gray and white fur was no longer shiny and her green eyes no longer bright. She spent her days in the overstuffed chair she had appropriated for herself. At least that's what she did until the fateful day the veterinarian started supplementing her with fluids. She immediately appeared healthier and moved more easily. Friends would say, "What happened to Henrie? She looks like a young cat." I told them it was the fluids. They'd ask for a glass of water.

Our bodies are a surprising 70 percent water, and we need to drink at least a quart of it every day—even more when it's hot, during exercise, or in a dry climate or dry atmosphere, like an airplane's. You probably won't feel thirsty every time you need to drink. Most of us have downplayed our water needs for so long that our thirst mechanism doesn't work as well as it ought to. Interestingly, if you gradually work up to six or eight glasses of water every day, your thirst response will become more reliable.

Drinking "liquids" won't do. Although herbal tea, freshly extracted vegetable juice, and diluted fruit juice can count in the water tally, coffee, tea, colas, and alcoholic beverages actually dehydrate the body. They're wet, but they're not water; in fact, they're *anti*water.

Lack of water stresses us no less than it does our houseplants. At the cellular level, dehydration makes us as droopy as a neglected philodendron. We need water to maintain proper fluid balance, for brain and kidney function, and to rid the body of waste materials. This makes it indispensable in keeping the body purified, so it's a fitting vehicle for spiritual practice. Drinking ample water is also necessary to keep the skin, which constantly loses moisture to the environment, soft and clear. Without enough moisture, the sebum-water balance in the skin is upset, which can cause breakouts. And lack of moisture in faces causes wrinkles the way lack of moisture in grapes causes raisins.

Water is also a safe, cheap, and effective appetite suppressant. Often when we think we're hungry, we're really thirsty. This is because the brain requires both water and sugar, and we can confuse the signals it sends us. The next time you think you're hungry but you ate not long ago, drink instead. If your body wants water, you'll be satisfied. If not, eat something.

Our society has reached such a level of artificiality that it's not uncommon to hear someone say, "I just don't like water." That's like saying, "I don't care much for air." If you find that water is too boring to drink in the quantity you ought to, make lemon water by putting one or two lemons and the juice you've squeezed from them into a quart of water. Keep one pitcher on your desk, another in the fridge.

You can get into the habit of carrying a bottle of water when you walk or drive. If it's there, you're more likely to drink it. Start with half-liter bottles; they're small enough that you'll finish them. You can refill them from your filtered or purified water source at home. "Designer water" may be a little silly, but as my daughter commented at thirteen: "Water just tastes better if it's in the right bottle."

You might also follow the advice of Ayurvedic doctors and sip warm water, either with lemon or straight, throughout the day. Gulping large quantities at meals is not a good idea since it can dilute the digestive juices, but Ayurveda teaches that sipping warm water while you're eating actually aids digestion. In addition to drinking water, help yourself stay hydrated by eating plenty of salads and juicy fruits, which have a high content of naturally purified water. Also, be sure there is enough moisture in your home and office air. You can measure the humidity level, which should be between 30 to 50 percent, with an inexpensive device called a hygrometer, available at any electronics store. If the air around you is dry, which is likely in the winter unless you have steam heat, consider purchasing a humidifier, at least for the bedroom. It can improve your complexion while you sleep.

Also for your skin's sake, think *dewy*. Put on moisturizer when your face or body is damp, so there will actually be some moisture for the lotion or cream to lock in. Choose steam baths over saunas. Spritz your face with a spray of spring water every hour or so when you're in a dry environment. And walk in the rain every chance you get. Soon after I married William, I ran outside to be part of an autumn rain shower. When I came back in, drenched and a little giddy, he handed me a towel and said, "I'll never figure you out, but I'll always love you."

44

Breathe the Best Air

*Sea breezes and mountain air didn't get their stellar
reputation for nothing, but just about any air that passes
as fresh is better than the unventilated indoor stuff.*

Air is our primary food, and nothing affects body, mind, and spirit as clearly, constantly, and profoundly as breathing. Physically, metabolism depends on oxygen. Without enough of it, our cells aren't able to function the way they're supposed to. You could eat an exemplary diet, but without sufficient oxygen, you wouldn't be able to use the nutrients it provides. Breathing also enables the body to rid itself of waste products, notably carbon dioxide. Oxygen is the supreme detoxifier.

Mental functioning is oxygen dependent as well. The brain, relative to its size, requires more oxygen than any other organ. This is why deep breathing is a first-line defense against stress. It's also part of the reason that you feel so good after doing

aerobic (oxygen-using) exercise: your brain just got a heaping helping of its favorite substance.

The breath is also the connecting point between our material and spiritual aspects. The calming effects of slow, steady breathing make it an integral part of meditative practices, although the connection was virtually lost here in the West until recent times. Thousands of years ago, Indian sages devised ways to work with the breath that they called *pranayama,* prana being the subtle life energy that flows through the body. They found that mastering *prana* had vitalizing, healing effects. The Chinese had discovered this, too, naming the invisible energy *chi*. This is what acupuncturists seek to manipulate with their treatments and martial artists learn to control through their disciplines.

With all the boons of breathing, you owe it to yourself to get the best air available. Sea breezes and mountain air didn't get their stellar reputation for nothing, but just about any air that passes as fresh is better than the unventilated indoor stuff. So go outside, or at least open a window. Yes, there is pollution from traffic and industry, but outdoor air is almost invariably cleaner than what we're breathing indoors, where we spend most of our time. In addition, choose some of the following ways to give yourself superior air:

Get out in nature. When you have the chance, get yourself to the woods, the mountains, the shore. And whenever you can, go to a park or anyplace you know of where trees outnumber cars.

Purify your indoor air. Houseplants are natural air purifiers. English ivy, ferns, aloe vera, chrysanthemum, and spider plants are particularly fond of turning toxicity into clean air, but all

plants are helpful. If you have allergies, or just a stubbornly dusty house, investing in a heavy-duty portable air filter, at least for the bedroom, is also a good idea.

Cut down on dust. You'll have cleaner air to breathe (and your skin and hair will stay cleaner longer) if you go barefoot indoors; shoes bring in much of the dirt and many of the contaminants that find their way into the air. Alternatively, install sizable mats at every entrance and place them lengthwise so they'll do some good even for people who don't wipe their feet. If you have carpets, a HEPA (that stands for "high efficiency particulate air") filter on your vacuum will keep dust and dirt from flying through the air. And unless you're lucky enough to have steam heat—which can help you to both softer skin and cleaner air—counteract the dust that a forced-air furnace sends out with a high-quality electrostatic filter, changed on schedule.

Use natural products. We pollute our own environments with the household cleaners and chemicals most of us regard as normal and necessary. There are far gentler versions of these products at natural foods stores. They work just as well as the harsh alternatives and will make your lungs your friends for life. You can also do a lot of cleaning with baking soda (mildly abrasive), distilled vinegar (disinfects), and dishwashing liquid (dissolves dirt).

If you have to pollute, by all means dilute. Open windows when you use a strong cleaner, paint, or even when you polish your nails. Let the fresher air from outside lessen the amount of toxins you breathe. Wherever you are, if fumes are giving you a headache, it's your body saying, "Get me out of here."

And every now and then when it comes to mind, give your breathing a little thought. Slow down if you're stressed or tense, and do the three-part breathing described in chapter 18, "Speak with Your True Voice." If you can even do three slow, deep breaths, you'll find yourself calmer, more centered, and more in control than you were just three breaths before. You can use your mind with your breathing, too. Think of breathing in peace, happiness, or courage—whatever you need at the moment—and exhaling anxiety, sadness, or fear. This is not a panacea, but it is a tool that can lift a mood or alter an attitude. Much of the time, we don't really need more than that.

PART VIII

Nurturing Your Spirit

45

Dedicate Your Life

Destiny and temperament determine the size of the stage;
you yourself determine the quality of the performance.

Women who rise above the crowd have standards higher than the crowd's; their lives are not solely their own but are invested in something larger. *Dedication, consecration,* and *surrender* are interchangeable terms that apply to the metamorphosis from a self-centered to a higher-centered way of being. This dedication can be to the God of your understanding or to some other spiritual or philosophical ideal. It might be to an art form, a life's work, a humanitarian cause, or some customized combination. The point is to connect with something greater than personal concerns and subsequently go about your daily tasks with more energy, commitment, and purpose.

Dedicating your life is also the surest way to change the world, or at least part of it. You can't shine your brightest in a world that's going on twenty-five watts. When you put effort and energy into what you believe in, you're using the power of your inner light to effect change for the better, not only within yourself but all around you. Some people are called to large efforts in the world, others to large efforts on a smaller scale. Destiny and temperament determine the size of your stage; you yourself determine the quality of the performance.

The very act of dedication lifts you above wherever you are when you start. Emerson wrote that people come in three classes. The first is the commonsense group; they're concerned with the health and financial well-being of themselves and those close to them. The next group he defined by their taste; they are committed to art or science, either as participants or supporters. Those in the third class, Emerson wrote, have spiritual perception. They "live above the beauty of the symbol to the beauty of the thing signified." Once in this category, you're free to enjoy the pleasures of all three. Nothing can elevate you from level one to two to three as surely or as rapidly as dedication to an ideal.

Fortunately, you don't have to dedicate your entire life all at once. Even people who join monastic orders take their vows one at a time. For the rest of us, dedicating our lives today and dealing with tomorrow when it gets here is good enough. An effective exercise is to remind yourself first thing upon awakening that this day, just this one, you're going to dedicate to a higher purpose. You can then offer your day to that purpose, with a prayer or a promise or whatever best solidifies your resolve.

Then you go about the fascinating business of spending twenty-four hours on earth. But as you do, you'll have the knowledge that this isn't just "another day, another dollar." It's more like "another day, another miracle." It's all in how you look at it.

I used to have a friend who did this exercise, dedicating her life each morning, as conscientiously as anybody could. After doing it for some time, she concluded, "I don't always do God's will, but I always want to." The desire to express the highest and best that's in you—through your work in the world, your relationships with others, what you make of your talents and your intelligence—is what invites your highest and best to come to the surface.

With it comes a host of dividends: strength, protection, and opportunities. You have a silent backer you may not have realized was there. You know how they sometimes call the person who puts up the money for a movie or a Broadway show an *angel?* It's something like that. Before, you may have been justifiably proud of standing on your own two feet. Your two feet are still there and still valuable, but when you dedicate your life, you also get wings.

46

Trust the Process

Trust is not fatalism or rolling over and playing dead.
It's experiencing life with the conviction that there
is more to it than meets the eye.

Have you ever had the experience that a book with a message for you seems to almost jump off the shelf at the library or the store? That happened for me with a tiny volume called *Trust Yourself to Life* by Clara Codd. Until I saw it, I hadn't realized how much I needed that message: Trust yourself to life. I think I exhaled fully for the first time in weeks by simply reading the title. It's okay, I was reminded, not to know what's coming next. Uncertainty need not be terrifying, and the vast majority of days are not tragic.

It's easier to trust if you have a worldview in which good is a greater force than evil—or even that good is the only force—and that what appears evil is simply lack of good, the way darkness is nothing except the absence of light. This can be difficult for anyone who has lived through anguish or who is sensitive enough to share in others' pain. The idea that good is all there is, or even that it is the mightier of two forces in play, might seem to diminish the reality of their suffering. It need not. People hold many opinions about why earth isn't paradise and why humans aren't angels. All we know for sure is that it isn't and we're not. Sometimes we bring suffering on ourselves, ignorantly or with full knowledge. Other times it comes from nowhere we can see and makes no sense whatsoever. Trust is believing that there is something else going on that we cannot fathom. It's not fatalism or rolling over and playing dead. It's experiencing life with the conviction that there is more to it than meets the eye.

Developing trust, or faith if you prefer the more theological term, is not something you can foist upon yourself by act of will. That usually doesn't even work for giving up chocolate, much less for putting your life into the care of some invisible force you may not be altogether sure exists. What you can do, however, if this seems like a monumental prospect, is not force it but *allow* it. *Allow* implies stepping aside, getting out of your own way. Trust to the degree you can, and see how it sits with you. Observe how it affects your life.

Some people have a rock-solid faith, based either on religious teachings or on some transforming experience most human beings don't get. Nevertheless, a woman who trusts—in the God of her understanding or simply in "the process"—often reveals an ease about her life and a grace about her bearing. She accepts the existence of variables, extenuating circumstances, and life's penchant for taking its own turns. There is an appealing sense of *yielding* in someone who has let go of the need to micromanage her own life. She still makes plans and works hard to bring them about, but she is just not as attached as the next person to a specific outcome. This leaves her with more opportunities to experience joy.

47

Memorize Words of Inspiration

Although not widely known or practiced, memorizing
snippets of beautiful words can bring powerful healing.

Wʜᴇɴ you program your mind with uplifting words, you
have them to draw on when you need them. Just hearing
or reading such words is helpful, but committing some to memory makes them yours. You can start with something short and
work up to longer passages. These can be quotations, poems,
songs, prayers, or scripture from your own tradition or somebody else's. When these words take the place of negative, cynical messages in your head, it's like having an attitude transplant.
And because body, mind, and soul are so intimately connected,
the change will affect all three.

One of my elementary school teachers insisted that her students memorize poems. The last half hour of every day she

would go to the back of the room and sit at a table that was too short for her legs, and anyone who had learned a poem could join her there to quietly recite it. I loved those private minutes, while the rest of the class worked on assignments, when it was my turn to repeat, "I wandered lonely as a cloud . . ." or even "Grow old along with me, the best is yet to be . . ." It sounded right to me, too, even though I didn't think much about growing old when I wasn't even young yet.

As I did get older, I added to my memorized repertoire. It wasn't just poetry anymore. There were passages of scripture: the Bible, the Bhagavad-Gita, the Dhammapada. I learned out-of-context quotations from Rousseau and Goethe and Emerson. And even the wisdom of coffee mugs and bumper stickers: "A well-behaved woman seldom makes history." "God grant me the serenity to put up with my blessings."

Because my brain can't hold everything, these memorized sentiments make room for themselves by edging out fearful thoughts, old griefs, and resentments. And when I'm alone or worried or sad, they come to the surface. It's like being personal friends with the wise thinkers of the ages. I'm privileged to invite them over on short notice and have them actually show up. Their thoughts get me out of my own when mine are negative or unproductive.

Memorization is rapidly becoming a lost art. Children in school rarely have to do it anymore. The rationale is, "It's on the Internet; they can just look it up." What has been forgotten is that something on the Internet or between the covers of a book, but not in your memory bank, is merely available *to* you. Something you commit to memory is part *of* you. That is a critical difference.

Although not widely known or practiced, memorizing snippets of beautiful words can bring powerful healing. Memorization is also an unsurpassed technique for exercising your brain and staying mentally sharp. (Winston Churchill attributed his skill as an extemporaneous speaker to the fact that he had committed to memory thousands of lines of verse.) Have fun with this. Select passages to memorize that speak to your soul. Start with something you're already familiar with and would like to know better or something you did memorize once—the Twenty-third Psalm, maybe, or the Prayer of St. Francis or one of Shakespeare's sonnets. You may be surprised by how much of it you still recall.

Or find something new, something that is meaningful to you today. Pick a poem, or a piece of one, and make it yours. Take its beauty into yourself and make it your beauty. Facilitate the process by copying it in your journal or in a spiral notebook earmarked for the purpose. This way you'll not only memorize quotations that will become your friends, you'll also create a private book of the poems, prayers, and passages that speak to your soul. It's easier to memorize something you write down. For this purpose, a pen works better than a keyboard; an unparalleled connection between the hand and the brain comes with writing longhand.

Put "wonderful words of life" into your life. When you have several quotations at your command, share them. And share your favorites repeatedly, especially with children. Then they can tell their children, "My mom used to say . . . ," or "This wonderful lady who lived next door when I was little always said. . . ." You can create a legacy from your own wise words and borrowed ones.

48

Respect Who You Are and
What You Value

In a desperate attempt to fit in, we sometimes deny
ourselves and what we believe in. This is damaging because
our inner beauty, our inner light, can't even find us when
we're masquerading as somebody else.

When you respect who you are and what you value, you issue an invitation to your inner beauty to show itself in every aspect of your life. You take care of yourself by seeking out supportive friends, frequenting inspiring places, and engaging in activities with which you strongly resonate. You stay in shape spiritually by stretching to do your best work and living by your highest ideals. You're comfortable within yourself because you have certain inviolable standards. There are some things you do and some things you don't, regardless of time, place, or circumstances. You are flexible and accommodating, but your core values are not up for compromise. As a result, you are at peace with yourself and with the world. You have energy to spare. And you shine like the dickens.

The tale of the Ugly Duckling is about the importance of self-respect. The ducks in that story thought the little swan was homely because they didn't understand the beauty of a swan— you know, the long neck thing. We often get ourselves in the same situation as that out-of-place cygnet. In a desperate attempt to fit in, we sometimes deny ourselves and what we believe in. This is damaging because our inner beauty, our inner light, can't even find us when we're masquerading as somebody else. In trying to be just one more duck, we cannot win. We either succeed in the charade and lose ourselves or fail at it and lament our inability to be like everybody else. This seeming failure is really a blessing, though. It shows that something in us is not allowing us to abandon our true self. Lucky break.

If you find that you're not fitting in as a duck, respect the fact that you are a swan. You're an individual. Being an individual is safe but sometimes solitary. That's why it's important to look for people with whom you feel comfortable, other "swans" who will reflect yourself back to you and show you how fully acceptable you are. The swan in the story was convinced that he was an ugly duckling until he saw other swans. You can meet some by joining groups or taking classes where you know there will be people with common interests, or you can just keep your eyes open. If you see someone at a coffeehouse who is reading a book you loved when you read it, say hello. You may not become best friends, but you could spend ten minutes with a soul sister, and that's worth something.

People who are cut from the same cloth seem to congregate in certain places. I feel surrounded by like-minded people when I'm in New York City. It seems to love writers. A lot of us are there, and it's where I do my best work. It is a definite advantage to be where you feel exquisitely at home. Nevertheless, the universe doesn't put anybody anywhere that there are no kindred spirits. I once lived in a little cabin in the southern Missouri Ozarks seven miles from the nearest town. Believe me, if I had been trying to find a place where few people thought like me, I would have found it there. I arrived as a spiritually eclectic vegetarian in a community full of pickup trucks, hunting rifles, and tent revivals. I thought I'd die of loneliness in a month. Instead, I made a close circle of friends, and it took only two weeks. (News travels fast in the Ozarks.) These women held many of my views and left alone the ones they didn't. Three of them are still my close friends today, over a decade after I left there.

When you find yourself in the midst of a value system that doesn't suit you—as you might in business, in your neighborhood, or even with family members—it helps to talk to people who share your values. It is also critical to your integrity that you assert your value system—not *on* others but *for* yourself. I saw an example of this recently when my daughter had a couple of actor friends, young women in their twenties, as houseguests. One of them located the nearest Catholic church and arranged to get herself to Mass on Sunday morning and meet the others later. She did this with such grace, not expecting anyone's help in being true to herself, simply doing it. This is how self-respect manifests in our daily dealings: quietly, unobtrusively, but significantly just the same.

In order to respect who you are and what you value, you have to know who you are and what you value today. What are your priorities? What makes you happy? How often do you actually do what makes you happy? When did you last feel genuinely content? What were you doing? Who were you with? What legacy, or legacies, do you want to leave the world? Remind yourself periodically of what gives your life joy and what gives it meaning. Never get too far from either of these.

Respect who you are by giving yourself permission to break free from the flock, even if just in tiny choices like where you'll go for breakfast or what you'll do with a free Saturday afternoon. And respect what you value by having standards that stick, when it's convenient and when it's not. People will notice, but that's the least of it.

49

Be Ready for Light Times

*Part of connecting with our inner light is being on the
lookout for glory days and rising to the occasion.*

Light times are when you get so much inner wealth you
can store some for later. These periods are the spiritual
equivalent of a bonus or a dividend check. You don't get one
every day, so when you do it's special. Generally speaking,
light times are when things go so well it's as if you're in a
bubble of goodness that nothing else can penetrate. But sometimes they come in the midst of crisis, when even with despair
all around you, you know you're protected, safe, and in
divine company. These states of grace can be spiritual experiences or earthly adventures. Either way, you get some exuberance out of them, and exuberance, said William Blake, *is*
beauty.

You've had light times already, and remembering them will help you to be available when the next one shows up. When I was pregnant with my daughter, I had nine months of light time. Even through morning sickness, the mingled feelings of humility and pride put a sunny spin on almost every aspect of my life. Seven years later I went hiking with this child in the Na Pali cliffs on Kauai. It was like being in God's living room. The light lasted weeks. And meeting William six years after that, even though I was a widow in my forties and supposedly too mature for the giddy elements of romance, put me in light mode for a year.

Bring some of your light times to mind. Maybe it was when you went to college or got your first apartment or took a special trip. Maybe it was when you discovered some new truth for yourself or about yourself, when you broke away from a limiting life choice into a broader one, or when you met the lover or teacher or friend who opened up your world as effortlessly as you open the shades in the morning.

The timing and frequency of these experiences depend on a combination of factors that probably range from the positions of the stars to the chemicals in your brain. Some light times you earn through past actions, and others you attract by vibrating at a frequency that draws them to you. However such phases enter your life, they are of value only when you realize what you've got. Otherwise, they're diverted elsewhere or diluted down to a nice day instead of a magical interlude.

The sad fact is that all of us have let light times pass us by because we weren't receptive to them. Part of connecting with our inner light is being on the lookout for these glory days and rising to the occasion. You do this by (1) expecting them, (2) preparing for them, and (3) showing gratitude in advance. Expect light times by remembering that you are a light being and understanding that you can do what you came here for only with a little help from heaven. You're not asking to be singled out for favors; you're simply acknowledging that you need some light times to get your work done, the way a mechanic needs a wrench or a carpenter needs a saw.

Prepare for light times by being ready physically, mentally, and spiritually. When purifying your body, elevating your thoughts, and acknowledging your spirit become a matter of course in your daily life, you'll be able to see light times coming and never miss another one.

Be grateful for the intervals when you're touched with an extra light. Your gratitude causes them to proliferate. Even if it feels that your last light time was ages ago, appreciate that one and the one that is sure to come. Say thanks for every day that's dazzling, every day that's good enough, and every day that you just make it through. Something else is always on the way. Life is composed of circles and cycles. Your spiritual practice and every snippet of wisdom you collect along the way direct your life in an upward spiral, even when setbacks make it seem otherwise. Light times are coming. Be ready to welcome them.

50

Look for Connections

Once you do a trial run of living your life based on a belief
in oneness instead of a belief in separateness,
nothing will ever be the same.

When you look for connections between yourself and other people, you find them. When you look for connections between yourself and animals, nature, and even ideas, you find connections there, too. And you find something else: the Infinite. Walt Whitman described it this way:

> I see something of God each hour of the twenty-four,
>   and each moment then,
> In the faces of men and women I see God,
>   and in my own face in the glass. . . .

In seeing the divine connection, he saw the divine in himself. But Whitman was a mystic, one of those rare human beings blessed with an experiential knowledge of the oneness of all life. Without that assurance, we can ponder the premise that we are all made of the same divine substance and, as such, part of some aggregate greatness. Whitman and the other mystics of all ages and cultures didn't have to think about it. They entered into a state of consciousness in which they knew it.

Mystics are lucky: their doubts are removed. The rest of us need to look for the connections, even if we bring our doubts along. Consider for the sake of argument that the mystics have a point, that indeed "no man is an island," that we are all made of the same light and united by the same love. Their assertion is of a world as Plato described it: "a single living entity containing all other living entities, which by their nature are related."

Grand as it all sounds, most of us know plenty of people we don't even like, much less wish to be related to. I wanted no part of this oneness business when I first heard a variation on the theme back in high school. My friend Rita, consummate fourteen-year-old intellectual, once posited, "What if you're only a molecule in God's knee?" I was appalled, fiercely independent as I believed I was, even though someone else was paying the bills and my only obligation was homework. I wasn't a part of anything, I told Rita: I *was* a thing, a universe unto myself. Of course, when no one asked me to the spring dance, I felt more like a speck than a universe.

Then I discovered the mystics. There were mystical poets like Rumi and William Blake; religious mystics like Martin Buber and Teilhard de Chardin; and the ones I related to most, women mystics: Myrtle Fillmore, Peace Pilgrim, St. Teresa. It didn't matter that

I was young; some of them were younger. They wrote about "greater life" and "boundless being." For a long time, I loved what I read and lived the way I always had. But as years passed, that started feeling uncomfortable. Being human, I changed as little as necessary to make the discomfort go away, but even small changes made a difference. I started talking less about other people, because all of a sudden it seemed that, if we're really all one, "going behind somebody's back" is pretty silly. And I became more respectful toward the "invisible people" that I'd formerly felt justified in disregarding: telephone solicitors, the bodies that made up a crowd, the street people to whom I'd often given a dollar but seldom a minute.

As a result, my life became a little less convenient and a lot more authentic. It was a good trade because I felt I didn't have to struggle so hard to get my share. Because I was more often happy for other people, I got to spend more time being happy. And as I saw more light in everybody else, I seemed to have more myself.

With an increased sense of connectedness, you will become more sensitive to the needs of others because you'll see that others are just you with different faces, each one an image of the Divine. Once you establish your life on a belief in oneness instead of a belief in separateness, you'll almost never be lonely. And although you might remember when you felt unattractive or unworthy, you won't feel that way anymore.

ACKNOWLEDGMENTS

Thanks to my agent and friend, Patti Breitman, who met me as a writer, turned me into an author, and models soul beauty in everything she does.

Thanks to my editor, Liz Perle, for her deft editing and good humor; and to publisher Stephen Hanselman and everyone else at Harper San Francisco for believing in *Lit from Within* and making me part of the Harper family.

Thanks to my foreign rights agent, Linda Michaels, who gives me the world; and publicists Meryl Zegarek and Calla Devlin for telling the world about this book.

Thanks to Jerrold Mundis and Crystal Leaman for keeping my writing on track, Martha Childers for research materials, Leslie Levine for moral support, and Pam Grout for access to her unpublished manuscript, "Think and Grow Beautiful."

To everyone who met with me about this project, answered an e-mail, provided insights, or attended a brainstorming session for *Lit from Within,* a sincere thank-you for your wisdom and generosity. There is no way I could have done this without every one of you.

And to my family, thank you for once again sharing me with a book. Your love and support are on every page.

FOR FURTHER READING

Barnard, Neal, MD. *Eat Right, Live Longer: Using the Natural Power of Foods to Age-Proof Your Body.* New York: Crown, 1997.

Berry, Carmen Renee, and Juanita Ryan. *Coming Home to Your Body: 365 Simple Ways to Nourish Yourself Inside and Out.* Berkeley: PageMill Press, 1996.

Carlson, Kris. *Don't Sweat the Small Stuff for Women.* New York: Hyperion, 2001.

Codd, Clara. *Trust Yourself to Life.* Wheaton, IL: Theosophical Publishing House, 1989.

Halbreich, Betty, Sally Wadyka, and Jeffrey Fulvimari. *Secrets of a Fashion Therapist: What You Can Learn Behind the Dressing Room Door.* New York: Cliff Street Books, 2000.

Hellmiss, Margot, and Falk Scheithauer. *Purify Your System for Health and Beauty.* New York: Sterling Publishing, 1998.

Jones, Susan Smith, PhD. *Choose to Live Peacefully.* Berkeley: Celestial Arts, 1999.

Joseph, Arthur Samuel. *The Sound of Your Soul: Discovering the Power of Your Voice.* Encino, CA: The Vocal Awareness Institute, 1996.

Masline, Shelagh Ryan, and Barbara Close. *Aromatherapy: The A to Z Guide to Healing with Essential Oils.* New York: Dell, 1997.

McBryde, Linda, MD. *The Mass Market Woman: Defining Yourself as a Person in a World That Defines You by Your Appearance.* Eagle River, AK: Crowded Hour Press, 1999.

Melina, Vesanto, RD, Brenda David, RD, and Victoria Harrison, RD. *Becoming Vegetarian: The Complete Guide to Adopting a Healthy Vegetarian Diet.* Summertown, TN: Book Publishing Company, 1995.

Moran, Victoria. *Creating a Charmed Life: Sensible, Spiritual Secrets Every Busy Woman Should Know.* San Francisco: HarperSanFrancisco, 1999.

Sachs, Melanie. *Ayurvedic Beauty Care: Ageless Techniques to Invoke Natural Beauty.* Twin Lakes, WI: Lotus Press, 1994.

Sinnige, Jacqueline. *Spiritual Beauty Care: Techniques and Practices to Enhance Your Inner and Outer Beauty.* Twin Lakes, WI: Lotus Press, 1997.

Sivananda Yoga Center. *Yoga, Mind and Body.* New York: DK Publishing, 1998.

Wolf, Naomi. *The Beauty Myth: How Images of Beauty Are Used Against Women.* New York: Anchor Books, 1992.

To contact the author, or enquire about a speaking engagement for your organization or personal coaching, visit her Web site, www.victoriamoran.com.